BUILDING AN EMPIRE

Building an Empire

BILL VINCENT

CONTENTS

Introduction: The Rise of Donald J. Trump as a Bus

Donald J. Trump's name is synonymous with opulence, luxury, and ambition. Long before his foray into politics, Trump established himself as a larger-than-life figure in the world of real estate and branding. His rise to fame as a businessman did not happen overnight—it was the result of a bold vision, relentless determination, and a knack for turning even the most challenging situations into opportunities. While many see Trump's skyscrapers, hotels, and casinos as the defining markers of his success, there is much more to the story of how he built his empire.

Born into a family steeped in real estate, Trump had the advantage of learning from his father, Fred Trump, who had already established himself as a successful developer in New York's outer boroughs. Fred Trump's focus on building affordable housing in Brooklyn and Queens laid the foundation for Donald's interest in property development. However, as the younger Trump entered adulthood, it became clear that his ambitions stretched far beyond the work his father had done. Donald was determined to make his mark in the heart of Manhattan, where prestige and high stakes went hand in hand.

In this introduction, we will explore the early influences that shaped Donald Trump's business mindset and how he turned his inherited real estate fortune into a global empire. From bold moves in Manhattan real estate to his eventual expansion into international markets, Trump has consistently demonstrated an ability to seize opportunities where others saw only risk. His rise in the 1970s and 1980s coincided with an era of financial boom, allowing him to leverage high-profile deals that captured the attention of the media and the public. But Trump's success has never been solely about property; it has been about brand, perception, and the art of the deal.

Trump's business philosophy revolves around a few core principles: think big, take calculated risks, and never shy away from self-promotion. Over the course of his career, these principles have allowed him to navigate the highs and lows of business with resilience. Whether negotiating multimillion-dollar real estate deals or licensing his name to a wide variety of products, Trump has turned his personal brand into an asset that transcends industries. His ventures have included not only real estate but also casinos, golf courses, television, and consumer products. This diversification has enabled Trump to maintain relevance in a fast-paced and ever-changing business world.

Throughout this book, we will focus on the milestones that have defined Trump's business career. We will look at his entry into the Manhattan real estate market, the construction of the now-iconic Trump Tower, his expansion into global markets, and the strategies that made *The Apprentice* one of the most successful reality television shows of all time. We will also examine the lessons Trump learned from both his successes and his setbacks, from the heights of prosperity to the challenges of navigating bankruptcy and financial restructuring.

What sets Donald Trump apart from many other business magnates is his ability to turn adversity into advantage. His career has been marked by risk-taking, but it is also underpinned by a keen understanding of branding and a relentless drive to stay in the public eye. For Trump, business is not just about making deals; it's about creating a lasting image and a legacy that will endure. As you read this book, you'll gain insight into the mind of a man who built one of the most recognizable empires in the world by mastering both the art of the deal and the power of the brand.

This book is not an analysis of Trump's political career but a celebration of his entrepreneurial spirit. Whether you admire or criticize him, there's no denying that Trump has left an indelible mark on the business world. His empire, built over decades, stands as a testament to the success that comes with thinking big, acting boldly, and capitalizing on every opportunity. Welcome to the story of Donald J. Trump's business empire.

| 1 |

Chapter 1: Roots in Real Estate

The Trump Family Legacy in Real Estate

Donald Trump's story as a business mogul begins not with him, but with his father, Fred Trump—a man whose vision, work ethic, and approach to real estate laid the foundation for the empire his son would later expand. Fred Trump, born in 1905, was the child of German immigrants and grew up in a modest household in Queens, New York. From an early age, Fred exhibited an entrepreneurial spirit, and by the time he was 15, he had already begun developing a keen interest in construction and real estate. Little did anyone know, this teenager would soon build one of the largest real estate businesses in New York's outer boroughs, setting the stage for his son's later ambitions.

Fred Trump's real estate career officially began in the 1920s, during a time of rapid urban expansion in New York City. He started small, constructing single-family homes in Queens, catering to the burgeoning middle class. His early ventures were modest, but they were rooted in a fundamental principle: there would always be demand for affordable housing. Fred believed in building sturdy, functional homes that could be sold to working families at reasonable prices. His business wasn't flashy, but it was practical and profitable, generating steady income as he continued to reinvest in more developments.

What truly set Fred apart from other developers was his foresight and ability to capitalize on government programs. During the Great Depression, while many businesses were struggling to survive, Fred saw an opportunity. He began working with government contracts, building affordable housing and earning government subsidies for his developments. His strategic partnership with the Federal Housing Administration (FHA) enabled him to thrive even during difficult economic times. This ability to leverage government support would later become a central tenet in Donald Trump's business approach, as he too would learn the value of government incentives and tax breaks.

As World War II came to an end, Fred's business entered its golden era. With soldiers returning home and the need for housing at an all-time high, Fred capitalized on the housing boom of the postwar years. His company, Trump Management, began developing larger-scale projects, including apartment complexes in Brooklyn and Queens. He was now constructing not just homes, but entire communities, earning a reputation for building affordable, well-made housing for middle-income families. By the 1950s, Fred Trump had become one of the most successful real estate developers in New York, amassing a personal fortune while establishing his family's name as a major player in the industry.

Fred Trump's conservative approach to business—focusing on long-term stability and minimizing risk—became a hallmark of his success. He was cautious with debt, avoided speculative projects, and always prioritized cash flow. This strategy of focusing on lower-risk, high-demand properties like apartment buildings in stable neighborhoods allowed him to steadily grow his business without taking on excessive financial risk. Fred Trump was not a man who courted attention or controversy. His empire was built quietly, through diligent planning and practical business choices.

For Donald Trump, growing up in this environment was both a blessing and a lesson. From his earliest days, Donald was exposed to the world of construction, real estate negotiations, and deal-making. He saw firsthand how his father built his empire brick by brick, avoiding the flashy, high-risk deals that often brought down less experienced developers. But as much as Fred Trump's approach was a masterclass in steady growth, it was not enough for his ambitious son. Donald was not content to stay in the outer boroughs, developing apartments for middle-class tenants. He wanted more—more risk, more reward, and more visibility.

Still, it's impossible to tell the story of Donald Trump's success without understanding the powerful influence of his father. Fred Trump's legacy was not just in the buildings he constructed, but in the business acumen and work ethic he passed down to his son. It was in Fred's conservative yet shrewd business philosophy that Donald learned the importance of timing, opportunity, and leveraging resources—lessons he would later adapt to his own, more aggressive style.

As we move through Donald Trump's journey, it's clear that Fred Trump's roots in real estate set the stage for what would become one of the most iconic business empires in the world. The Trump name, already established in Brooklyn and Queens, was poised to reach even greater heights, as the son sought to build upon his father's foundation—but this time, in the heart of Manhattan.

Learning the Business: Donald Trump's Early Involvement

Donald Trump's introduction to the world of real estate came at an early age, and it was no accident. His father, Fred Trump, believed in teaching his children the value of hard work and, more importantly, how to manage and grow a business. From the time Donald was a teenager, he was closely involved in the family business, Trump Management, learning the intricacies of real estate development from the ground up. It was in these formative years that Donald began to absorb the lessons that would eventually shape his own career—lessons in negotiation, construction, finance, and management, all taught by a man who had mastered the art of property development.

Fred Trump was not the type of father who sheltered his children from the realities of business. By the age of 13, Donald was already visiting construction sites and office buildings, observing how his father handled contractors, negotiated deals, and managed properties. This early exposure to the business was invaluable, as it gave Donald a firsthand view of the complexities of real estate long before most young men his age were even thinking about their careers. These experiences were not just educational; they were formative, embedding in Donald a sense of ambition and a hunger for success that would fuel him in the years to come.

While his father's empire was based in the outer boroughs of New York, primarily in Brooklyn and Queens, Donald quickly recognized that the principles behind his father's success—identifying opportunities, managing risk, and understanding the market—were universal. He understood that real estate wasn't just about land and buildings; it was about creating value, spotting potential where others saw only risk, and knowing how to get deals done. These early lessons were absorbed through countless hours spent at his father's side, watching and learning.

Donald's formal education played a significant role in his business development as well. After attending the New York Military Academy, where he cultivated discipline and leadership skills, he enrolled at Fordham University before transferring to the prestigious Wharton School of Finance at the University of Pennsylvania. Wharton, renowned for producing top-tier business leaders, provided Donald with a strong foundation in economics and finance. But as valuable as his education was, it was the real-world experience with his father that truly prepared him for the business world. While at Wharton, Donald continued to work with his father during the summers, gaining deeper insights into the financial and managerial aspects of real estate development.

Upon graduating from Wharton in 1968, Donald immediately dove headfirst into the family business. His first official role in Trump Management involved overseeing the day-to-day operations of the company's extensive portfolio of properties. This included managing tenants, overseeing repairs, and dealing with the inevitable challenges that come with running a large real estate operation. For most young men, this would have been a daunting task, but Donald thrived in this environment. He had learned the importance of maintaining cash flow, managing costs, and ensuring that properties were kept in good condition—all lessons Fred had ingrained in him from the start.

But while Fred Trump's success came from developing low- to middle-income housing, Donald was already thinking bigger. He saw real estate as more than just a business of steady returns and government contracts. He saw it as a platform for growth, prestige, and influence. His time spent managing his father's properties only fueled his desire to break into Manhattan—a real estate market that was far riskier, more competitive, and infinitely more glamorous than the outer boroughs.

Still, Donald's early years working in the family business gave him an indispensable education. He learned how to negotiate tough contracts, how to work with banks and secure favorable financing, and how to deal with the myriad challenges that come with large-scale property management. He also learned the importance of understanding the market and anticipating trends, a skill that would prove crucial when he eventually set his sights on Manhattan's skyline.

One of the most important lessons Donald learned from Fred was how to navigate the often complex world of government regulations and financing. Fred Trump had mastered the art of working with the Federal Housing Administration (FHA) to secure favorable loans and subsidies for his developments, and Donald would take this knowledge and apply it in his own ventures. Understanding how to leverage government programs to maximize profits would later become a key strategy in Donald's approach to real estate.

But perhaps the most valuable lesson Donald learned in these early years was the importance of resilience. The real estate business, as Fred often reminded him, was not for the faint of heart. It required thick skin, persistence, and the ability to bounce back from setbacks. As Donald took on more responsibilities within the company, he quickly learned that not every deal went smoothly, not every tenant paid on time, and not every project was a success. But in the Trump family, failure was never final—it was simply a stepping stone to the next opportunity.

By the early 1970s, Donald had gained enough experience to start thinking about his own ventures. He had spent years learning the business from the inside out, honing his instincts and sharpening his skills. While his father's empire had been built on stability and slow, steady growth, Donald was ready for something bigger. The lessons learned during his early involvement with Trump Management would become the foundation upon which he would build his own empire—an empire that would soon extend far beyond the family's Brooklyn and Queens roots.

Differentiating from Fred: Donald's Manhattan Ambitions

By the early 1970s, Donald Trump had established himself as a rising force within the family business, Trump Management. His father, Fred Trump, had laid a solid foundation with his successful real estate developments in Brooklyn and Queens, but Donald had his eyes set on something much grander. For Donald, success in the outer boroughs wasn't enough; he wanted to play in the highest-stakes arena of all—Manhattan. The glitz, glamour, and prestige of Manhattan's towering skyscrapers captivated him, and he believed his future lay not in the stability of middle-class housing but in the high-profile, high-reward world of Manhattan real estate.

The contrast between father and son was stark. Fred Trump had always been conservative in his approach to business. He believed in building affordable housing in stable neighborhoods and shied away from the volatility and speculative nature of the Manhattan market. Fred's philosophy was simple: focus on cash flow, minimize risk, and avoid excessive debt. Donald, however, was drawn to the very elements of Manhattan that his father avoided—the glamour, the risks, the potential for massive rewards, and the attention that came with big, bold projects.

Donald's first step into the Manhattan market was not just a business decision but a declaration of independence from his father's way of doing things. He knew that if he could succeed in Manhattan, he would not only build his own reputation but would also set himself apart from Fred's more cautious approach. Manhattan was a world away from the working-class apartment buildings of Brooklyn and Queens. It was a place where fortunes could be made—or lost—on a single deal, where developers vied for prime pieces of real estate, and where every move was scrutinized by the media and the financial community.

In the early 1970s, New York City was struggling with financial instability and urban decay. Crime rates were high, many buildings in Manhattan were in disrepair, and the city was teetering on the edge of bankruptcy. For most developers, this was not the time to invest in Manhattan. The risks seemed too great, and the future of the city was uncertain. But Donald saw an opportunity. He believed that Manhattan's downturn was temporary and that those who invested during its lowest point would reap the rewards when the city inevitably bounced back. This was a pivotal moment in Donald's career—his decision to embrace risk, where others saw only failure, would become a hallmark of his business strategy.

Donald's ambitions were focused on the heart of Manhattan—the very symbol of power and prestige in the real estate world. He began searching for opportunities to make his mark, determined to secure a signature deal that would put him on the map. He quickly realized, however, that breaking into the Manhattan market would not be easy. For one, he lacked the track record in the city that would make banks comfortable lending him the massive amounts of capital required for such projects. Moreover, the established players in Manhattan real estate were hesitant to give a young, relatively untested developer a seat at the table.

But Donald was nothing if not persistent. He understood the importance of relationships in the world of real estate, and he set about building connections with key figures in New York's financial and political circles. He began networking aggressively, attending events, and cultivating relationships with bankers, politicians, and influential figures in the city. His charm, confidence, and vision for what Manhattan could become won over several powerful allies, including Roy Cohn, a prominent attorney and political fixer who would become a key advisor to Donald in his early years.

While Fred Trump had always been content to operate quietly behind the scenes, Donald recognized the power of visibility and media attention. He knew that in Manhattan, image mattered as much as substance, and he wasn't afraid to court publicity. Donald's bold personality and larger-than-life vision for the future made him stand out in a city filled with ambitious developers. He knew that if he could grab the attention of the press, he could create a perception of success that would open doors to the financing and opportunities he needed.

Donald's first real chance to break into the Manhattan market came with the Commodore Hotel. The once-grand hotel, located just next to Grand Central Station, had fallen into disrepair, a victim of the city's economic troubles. In the eyes of many, the hotel was a symbol of New York's decline—a faded relic of its former glory. But Donald saw potential. He believed that with the right vision and investment, the Commodore could be transformed into a world-class hotel that would not only revitalize the property but also help signal the resurgence of Manhattan itself.

However, the Commodore deal was far from simple. The building was owned by Penn Central, which had filed for bankruptcy, and any redevelopment would require extensive negotiations, not only with the bankrupt railroad but also with the city government and potential financial backers. Most importantly, it would require a substantial amount of capital—far more than Donald had access to at the time. But Donald was undeterred. He leveraged his connections and convinced the city of New York to provide tax abatements, which reduced the financial burden on the project and made it a more attractive investment for banks.

The successful acquisition and renovation of the Commodore Hotel would mark Donald's first major triumph in Manhattan. It was a deal that required creativity, persistence, and an ability to navigate complex political and financial landscapes—all qualities that would come to define Donald's approach to business. By the time the hotel reopened in 1980, rebranded as the Grand Hyatt, Donald had proven to himself and to the real estate world that he could play in the big leagues. The project was a resounding success, both financially and in terms of Donald's burgeoning reputation.

In Donald Trump's pursuit of Manhattan, the contrast with his father could not have been clearer. Fred Trump's business was built on stability and security, while Donald's vision was driven by ambition, risk, and a desire for visibility. Manhattan was a market that Fred had long avoided, but for Donald, it was the ultimate prize. The success of the Commodore deal solidified Donald's place in the Manhattan real estate scene and set the stage for the bold, high-profile projects that would come to define his career.

Key Early Deals: Swifton Village and The Commodore Hotel

Donald Trump's early real estate career was marked by two pivotal deals that helped establish his reputation as a bold, innovative developer with an appetite for risk and a talent for turning around failing properties. These deals—the acquisition and management of Swifton Village in Cincinnati, Ohio, and the redevelopment of The Commodore Hotel in Manhattan—would provide Donald with the experience, confidence, and credibility he needed to make his mark in the competitive world of New York real estate.

The first of these deals, Swifton Village, came in 1962, while Donald was still working closely with his father, Fred Trump. Swifton Village was a large, troubled apartment complex in Cincinnati. The property, consisting of over 1,200 units, had been built in the postwar boom but had fallen into disrepair by the time the Trumps acquired it. Its vacancy rates were high, maintenance had been neglected, and the neighborhood surrounding the complex had begun to deteriorate. To many, Swifton Village was a losing proposition, a failing asset that would be difficult to turn around.

For Fred Trump, the deal was a typical example of his conservative but effective approach to real estate. He had a history of buying distressed properties at a discount and methodically bringing them back to profitability through diligent management and repairs. This strategy had worked well for Fred in the outer boroughs of New York, and he believed it could be applied to Swifton Village. But while Fred oversaw the acquisition, it was Donald, fresh out of Wharton School, who was given significant responsibility in the project. This would be one of Donald's first opportunities to take a leadership role in a major development, and it was a test of his ability to manage a large-scale real estate turnaround.

Donald approached the challenge of Swifton Village with the same drive and ambition that would later define his career. He recognized that turning the complex around would require more than just basic repairs—it needed a comprehensive overhaul, both in terms of the physical property and its management. Under Donald's supervision, the Trump team invested heavily in refurbishing the units, improving the overall condition of the buildings, and implementing more efficient property management practices. Donald also understood the importance of marketing, and he worked to change the perception of Swifton Village in the local community, positioning it as a more attractive option for middle-income renters.

Within a few years, the efforts paid off. Occupancy rates at Swifton Village improved, and the complex returned to profitability. By 1972, Fred and Donald Trump were able to sell Swifton

Village for $6.75 million, a significant profit compared to its acquisition price. While the deal may not have attracted the attention that Donald would later crave, it was an important learning experience. Swifton Village taught Donald the value of taking on distressed properties and turning them into profitable ventures—a strategy he would employ repeatedly in the years to come. It also gave him a taste of the kind of larger-scale projects he would soon pursue on his own.

But while Swifton Village was a solid, if somewhat under-the-radar, success, it was The Commodore Hotel deal that would truly catapult Donald Trump into the spotlight. By the mid-1970s, Donald was ready to break away from the family's traditional focus on outer-borough housing and establish himself as a major player in Manhattan real estate. The Commodore Hotel, located next to Grand Central Station, represented the perfect opportunity. The hotel, once a symbol of New York City's grandeur, had fallen into severe disrepair. Its façade was crumbling, its occupancy rates had plummeted, and it was hemorrhaging money. Like Swifton Village, The Commodore was seen by many as a lost cause.

But Donald saw potential. He recognized that the hotel's prime location—just steps from one of the busiest transportation hubs in the city—gave it an inherent value that could be unlocked with the right vision. However, the deal was far more complex than anything Donald had previously tackled. First, the hotel was owned by the Penn Central Transportation Company, which had filed for bankruptcy. Negotiating with a bankrupt entity added an extra layer of difficulty, as any sale would need to be approved by the bankruptcy court. Second, the redevelopment of the hotel would require a massive amount of capital, far more than Donald or his father had access to at the time.

Undeterred, Donald began putting together a plan to bring the deal to life. He approached the Hyatt Corporation, a growing hotel chain that was looking to expand its presence in New York. Donald convinced Hyatt to partner with him on the redevelopment of The Commodore, offering them a share of the profits in exchange for their investment and hotel management expertise. But even with Hyatt on board, the financials of the deal were still shaky. This is where Donald's negotiation skills—and his ability to navigate political and financial systems—came into play.

Recognizing the importance of government support in making the deal viable, Donald approached the city of New York and pitched the redevelopment as a project that would not only revitalize the hotel but also serve as a catalyst for the broader rejuvenation of the area around Grand Central Station. New York City, struggling with economic woes and eager to attract investment, agreed to a tax abatement that would significantly reduce the financial burden on the project. This tax break was critical in making the deal attractive to lenders, and with the city's support secured, Donald was able to raise the necessary financing to move forward.

The renovation of The Commodore was a monumental undertaking, but under Donald's direction, it was transformed from a crumbling relic into a modern, luxurious hotel. When the Grand Hyatt, as it was rebranded, opened in 1980, it was an instant success. The hotel not only revived the fortunes of The Commodore but also helped ignite a broader resurgence in the surrounding area. For Donald, the deal was a defining moment. It proved that he could compete in the cutthroat world of Manhattan real estate, and it established his reputation as a dealmaker capable of pulling off complex, high-profile projects.

The Commodore Hotel deal was more than just a business success—it was a turning point in Donald Trump's career. It demonstrated his ability to take on high-risk ventures, his skill in navigating political and financial hurdles, and his flair for making a splash in the media. It was the first of many major Manhattan projects that would come to define his career, and it solidified his place as a rising star in New York's real estate scene.

Together, Swifton Village and The Commodore Hotel marked the beginning of Donald Trump's transition from a capable, if conventional, real estate developer into the bold, ambitious mogul he would soon become.

Expanding the Vision: Trump Tower and the Manhattan Skyline

The success of the Commodore Hotel in the late 1970s marked a significant turning point in Donald Trump's career, but it was only the beginning. Having proven he could transform a failing property into a high-profile success, Donald was now ready for his next, even more ambitious move—one that would forever change the skyline of New York City and solidify his status as a real estate mogul. This move came in the form of Trump Tower, the iconic skyscraper on Fifth Avenue that would become synonymous with the Trump brand and the centerpiece of his growing empire.

For Donald, the appeal of Trump Tower was not just its potential as a profitable real estate development but its symbolic value. He understood that real estate in Manhattan was as much about image as it was about money, and he wanted to make a statement—both about his personal ambitions and about what his brand could achieve. Trump Tower would be more than just another building; it would be a monument to his success and a visible declaration that Donald Trump had arrived as a major force in the world of real estate.

The site Donald had his eye on was the former Bonwit Teller department store, a well-known but aging building on Fifth Avenue between 56th and 57th Streets. Fifth Avenue was—and still is—one of the most prestigious shopping streets in the world, home to luxury retailers, high-end boutiques, and some of the most valuable real estate in Manhattan. The location was perfect for what Donald envisioned: a gleaming skyscraper that would combine luxury residential apartments, high-end retail space, and office units. It was a bold and unprecedented concept at the time—no one had ever built a tower that mixed residential and commercial spaces in such a prime location.

But securing the Bonwit Teller site was no small feat. The building was owned by Genesco, a company that was hesitant to sell the property. However, Donald's persistence, charm, and negotiation skills came into play once again. He approached the deal with the same tenacity that had driven the Commodore Hotel redevelopment, convincing Genesco that selling the property to him was the best way forward. In the end, Donald managed to acquire the site, setting the stage for one of the most iconic developments of his career.

Building Trump Tower required navigating a number of obstacles, not the least of which was the demolition of the historic Bonwit Teller building itself. While some preservationists wanted to save portions of the building's Art Deco façade, Donald made the controversial decision to demolish the entire structure to make way for his new vision. This decision drew criticism, but it also signaled a shift in Donald's approach to real estate: he was willing to break with tradition in order to create something bold, modern, and unmistakably his own.

As construction on Trump Tower began in 1979, Donald's ambitions for the project grew. He hired Der Scutt, a renowned architect, to design the building. Scutt's vision for Trump Tower was sleek, modern, and elegant—a shimmering bronze-glass tower that would rise 58 stories above Fifth Avenue. The design was innovative in its use of an atrium—a grand, marble-clad space that would serve as the centerpiece of the building, open to the public and filled with upscale shops and restaurants. The tower's residential units would be marketed as the epitome of luxury, featuring lavish interiors, sweeping views of Central Park, and the cachet of living in one of New York's most exclusive addresses.

One of the key factors that set Trump Tower apart from other developments was Donald's emphasis on branding. From the very beginning, he understood the power of the Trump name, and he made sure that it was prominently displayed everywhere—from the gleaming sign at the entrance to the gold-plated fixtures inside. Donald wanted everyone to know that Trump Tower wasn't just another high-rise; it was a symbol of success, luxury, and ambition. By branding the building with his own name, Donald was making a bold statement: he wasn't just a real estate developer; he was a brand.

The marketing campaign for Trump Tower was as ambitious as the project itself. Donald made sure that the media was involved every step of the way, turning the construction of the tower into a public spectacle. He courted journalists, gave exclusive tours of the construction site, and made sure that every milestone—from the completion of the atrium to the sale of the first residential unit—was covered in the press. By the time Trump Tower was completed in 1983, it was already one of the most talked-about buildings in New York.

When Trump Tower finally opened, it was an immediate success. The residential units sold at record prices, and the building's retail space attracted some of the biggest names in luxury retail. The tower quickly became a landmark, not just because of its prime location and striking design but because of what it represented: the arrival of a new kind of real estate mogul—one who wasn't afraid to take risks, embrace modernity, and build not just buildings but a personal brand.

The success of Trump Tower did more than just establish Donald Trump as a force in Manhattan real estate; it catapulted him into the public consciousness as a larger-than-life figure. For the first time, the Trump name became synonymous with luxury, success, and ambition on a national—and even international—scale. The tower itself became a tourist destination, drawing visitors from around the world who wanted to see the building that had become a symbol of the high-flying 1980s real estate boom.

But for Donald, Trump Tower was about more than just money or fame. It was a personal achievement that represented everything he had worked for—the culmination of his early lessons in real estate, his bold decision to move into Manhattan, and his vision for what the Trump brand could be. Trump Tower was more than just a building; it was a statement, one that announced to the world that Donald Trump was not just a developer but a visionary who had changed the landscape of Manhattan.

With the success of Trump Tower, Donald Trump's career entered a new phase. He had gone from being Fred Trump's ambitious son to one of the most recognized names in real estate, and his ambitions only grew larger. The tower on Fifth Avenue was the first of many high-profile projects that would come to define Donald's career in the 1980s and beyond. But Trump Tower remained, and still remains, the building that symbolized Donald Trump's arrival as a real estate mogul and a brand unto himself.

| 2 |

Chapter 2: Breaking into Manhattan

Setting His Sights on Manhattan

From an early age, Donald Trump had ambitions that extended far beyond his father's real estate holdings in Brooklyn and Queens. While Fred Trump built a substantial fortune by developing and managing affordable housing for middle-income tenants, Donald was captivated by the allure of Manhattan—the gleaming skyscrapers, the power and prestige of its elite, and the potential to make a name for himself in the heart of the world's greatest city. To Donald, Manhattan represented more than just business opportunities; it was the ultimate symbol of success, a stage where only the boldest and most ambitious could shine.

The contrast between Donald's aspirations and his father's conservative approach to real estate could not have been more pronounced. Fred Trump was a master of the outer boroughs, thriving in the world of post-war housing developments and working-class neighborhoods. He built and managed thousands of units, securing government contracts and taking advantage of tax incentives to build a reliable and profitable business. Fred's formula was simple: steady growth with minimal risk. He wasn't interested in the limelight or in taking big gambles; he was focused on providing affordable housing and earning a steady return on investment.

But for Donald, this model felt limiting. He respected his father's achievements but wanted to play on a bigger, more glamorous stage. While Fred was content to work behind the scenes, Donald craved visibility and recognition. The tall buildings, high-profile projects, and massive deals of Manhattan drew him like a magnet. As a young man, Donald often crossed the East River into Manhattan, marveling at the skyscrapers and imagining what it would be like to make his mark on the city. His ambitions were clear from the start: he didn't want to just be a successful real estate developer; he wanted to be *the* real estate developer, the one whose name would be synonymous with Manhattan's skyline.

Breaking into Manhattan real estate, however, was no small feat. The market was tightly controlled by established families and developers who had been operating in the city for generations. Manhattan was not a place for newcomers, especially not those from the outer boroughs. Donald was well aware of the skepticism he would face. Many Manhattan elites viewed the outer boroughs as provincial and second-rate, and they were not eager to let a young upstart from Queens play in their backyard. The real estate world in Manhattan was a closed, insular club, and Donald was an outsider.

But the very challenges that would have deterred others only fueled Donald's ambition. He saw Manhattan's exclusivity as a barrier worth breaking through, not something to be intimidated by. In fact, the harder it seemed to crack into the market, the more determined he became to succeed. Donald wasn't just interested in building a few buildings in Manhattan; he wanted to become a central figure in its real estate world. He understood that to succeed there, he would need to approach things differently—he couldn't simply follow his father's model. Manhattan required boldness, risk-taking, and a willingness to operate at a much larger scale.

Fred Trump, however, was skeptical. He knew Manhattan was a different beast than the outer boroughs, and he was wary of the risks involved in developing there. For Fred, the outer boroughs had been a goldmine of steady, low-risk opportunities, and he didn't see the need to gamble on Manhattan. His business was flourishing, and the thought of overextending into the volatile world of Manhattan real estate seemed unnecessary, even reckless. He also knew that Donald's ambitions were not just about money—they were about fame, influence, and legacy. While Fred was proud of his son's drive, he was concerned that Donald's desire for the spotlight might lead him to take on risks that could jeopardize the family's business.

Despite his father's reservations, Donald was undeterred. He believed that success in Manhattan would not only elevate his personal brand but also take the Trump family business to the next level. He recognized that Manhattan was where the biggest deals were made, where the most influential people lived, and where the media paid attention. If he wanted to build a name that would be remembered, it had to be in Manhattan.

The key for Donald was to identify an entry point—an opportunity that would allow him to break into the Manhattan market and prove himself. He understood that he couldn't simply waltz into the city and start buying up skyscrapers; he needed a project that would give him credibility, something big enough to capture attention but manageable enough for him to handle. Donald also knew that once he had a foothold, the rest of his ambitions could follow. Manhattan was a place where one big success could lead to many more, but first, he had to find that opening.

That opening came in the mid-1970s, during a time of economic crisis in New York City. The city was on the verge of bankruptcy, real estate prices were depressed, and many buildings were falling into disrepair. For established developers, this was a time of caution, but for Donald, it represented an opportunity. He saw the potential to acquire valuable properties at low prices and, with the right vision and execution, turn them into profitable ventures. The timing was fortuitous: Manhattan was in desperate need of investment, and Donald was eager to make his move.

It was a perfect storm of circumstances—a combination of ambition, market timing, and Donald's unrelenting drive to succeed—that would set the stage for his first major breakthrough in Manhattan real estate. While others saw only risk, Donald saw opportunity. Manhattan was calling, and Donald Trump was ready to answer.

Overcoming Skepticism from Manhattan's Elite

Breaking into Manhattan's tightly controlled real estate market was no easy task, and Donald Trump knew that better than anyone. The city's development scene was dominated by a small circle of established families and firms that had been entrenched for decades. These power brokers viewed Manhattan as their domain, and they weren't eager to welcome new players, especially a young, ambitious developer from Queens. Donald faced an immediate challenge: overcoming the skepticism of Manhattan's elite, who saw him as an outsider untested in the high-stakes world of big-city real estate.

Manhattan's elite didn't just include developers; it encompassed bankers, politicians, and influential figures who played crucial roles in financing and approving major projects. To succeed, Donald needed not only to build, but also to navigate the complex web of relationships and politics that underpinned New York City's real estate market. This was a world of personal connections, where who you knew was just as important as what you could do. Donald knew that he had to find a way to break into this network if he was going to make a name for himself in Manhattan.

The skepticism he faced was intense. To the seasoned real estate families of Manhattan, Donald was young and inexperienced, with a family business that was relatively modest by their standards. His father, Fred Trump, had built a reputation as a successful developer in Brooklyn and Queens, but Fred had deliberately stayed out of the Manhattan game, seeing it as too risky and unstable. To many, Donald's ambitions to conquer Manhattan seemed more like a brash dream than a credible plan.

But Donald was not one to be easily discouraged. He understood that in order to succeed, he had to break through this wall of skepticism and prove himself as more than just Fred Trump's son. He needed to demonstrate that he had the vision, the guts, and the business acumen to play on Manhattan's biggest stage. His strategy was to take bold, calculated risks and make deals that others were too cautious to pursue. He knew that if he could pull off a major success, the elite would no longer be able to ignore him.

One of the first major connections Donald made was with Roy Cohn, a notorious lawyer and political fixer who had built a career by navigating the complex and often murky world of New York power politics. Cohn, who had gained national attention as Senator Joseph McCarthy's chief counsel during the anti-Communist hearings of the 1950s, had become a key player in New York's business and political circles. He was known for his aggressive, no-holds-barred style, and he had a wide network of contacts that spanned the city's legal, financial, and political establishments.

Donald quickly realized that Cohn could be an invaluable ally as he sought to establish himself in Manhattan. While Cohn was a controversial figure, his influence was undeniable, and his ability to open doors was exactly what Donald needed. In Cohn, Donald found someone who shared his penchant for aggressive tactics and who was unafraid to ruffle feathers in the pursuit of success. The two struck up a close working relationship, and Cohn became one of Donald's most trusted advisors during the early years of his Manhattan rise.

Cohn's connections helped Donald gain access to important financial backers and political figures who could make or break real estate deals in the city. Through Cohn, Donald was able to secure introductions to key figures in New York's banking industry, which was essential for financing his ambitious projects. In the cutthroat world of Manhattan real estate, securing favorable financing terms was often the difference between success and failure, and Cohn's influence helped Donald negotiate deals that would have been out of reach for most young developers.

But Donald's relationship with Cohn wasn't just about connections—it was also about learning how to navigate the often brutal realities of New York's business world. From Cohn, Donald learned the value of fighting back aggressively against critics and opponents. Cohn's philosophy was simple: never back down, never apologize, and always be willing to go on the offensive. This approach resonated deeply with Donald, who admired Cohn's toughness and ability to thrive in a hostile environment. It was a lesson Donald would carry with him throughout his career, using the media and public opinion to his advantage while remaining unshaken by criticism.

As Donald's connections and confidence grew, he began to find his footing in the Manhattan market. He recognized that one way to gain acceptance from the city's elite was to align himself with projects that served the public good—projects that would not only turn a profit but also contribute to the revitalization of the city. This strategy became particularly important during the late 1970s, when New York was grappling with financial crises, urban decay, and a crumbling infrastructure. Donald realized that by positioning himself as someone who could help transform the city's fortunes, he could gain the support of key political and business leaders.

One of Donald's early tactics was to identify distressed properties that had fallen out of favor with other developers. These were often buildings that were either in financial trouble or suffering from years of neglect, but Donald saw potential where others saw risk. He knew that if he could turn these failing properties into successful ventures, it would validate his vision and force the city's power brokers to take him seriously. It was a high-risk strategy, but Donald was convinced that it would pay off.

Despite the skepticism he faced, Donald's persistence and ability to form strategic relationships began to pay off. Slowly but surely, he gained a reputation as a developer who was willing to take on difficult projects and who had the skills to make them work. He wasn't yet fully accepted by the Manhattan elite, but he was no longer seen as an outsider from Queens. Donald had proven that he could play in the big leagues, and with each deal, he moved closer to becoming a major force in Manhattan real estate.

This relentless drive to overcome skepticism and prove himself in the face of doubt would become one of the defining characteristics of Donald's career. For him, every hurdle was an opportunity, and every doubter was fuel for his ambition. He understood that success in Manhattan required more than just money and connections—it required perseverance, adaptability, and an unwavering belief in his own vision. Donald Trump had set his sights on Manhattan, and there was nothing that was going to stand in his way.

The Commodore Hotel Deal

Donald Trump's breakthrough into Manhattan's real estate world came in the form of a crumbling, nearly bankrupt property: the Commodore Hotel. Situated near Grand Central Station, the Commodore was once a grand symbol of luxury but had fallen into disrepair by the 1970s. Like much of New York City at the time, the hotel was a victim of the city's broader financial collapse and urban decay. But where others saw a dying building, Donald saw an opportunity. The Commodore Hotel became the key to his Manhattan empire and was the project that would catapult him from an ambitious outsider to a major player in the city's real estate scene.

The Commodore wasn't just any property. Its location was prime real estate, right in the heart of midtown Manhattan, but years of neglect had left it in a state of decay. Occupancy rates were low, and the hotel had lost its once-proud reputation. It was clear to most observers that the Commodore needed a complete overhaul, but given the high costs of such a renovation and New York's economic woes, no developer was willing to take on the challenge. This made it the perfect target for Donald Trump, who saw in the Commodore an opportunity to do what others couldn't—or wouldn't—do.

Donald's first step was securing the hotel's ownership. At the time, the Commodore was owned by the Penn Central Railroad, which was itself in bankruptcy. Donald knew that Penn Central was eager to offload the failing hotel, but securing the property wasn't just a matter of buying it outright. It required negotiating with both Penn Central and the city government, as well as navigating a labyrinth of legal and financial complexities. Donald's tenacity and deal-making skills were put to the test, but he was determined to make the Commodore his first major Manhattan success.

The real breakthrough came when Donald managed to secure a partnership with the Hyatt Corporation. He knew that to make the Commodore project work, he needed a partner with both the financial resources and the credibility to help him pull off the renovation. Hyatt, one of the largest hotel chains in the world, was looking to expand its presence in New York, and Donald saw the potential for a win-win partnership. He approached Hyatt's top executives with a bold proposal: if they agreed to partner with him on the Commodore, he would handle the redevelopment, and they would manage the hotel once it was completed. Hyatt, intrigued by the opportunity to enter the New York market, agreed to the deal.

With Hyatt on board, Donald's next challenge was securing financing for the project. This was no small task. Manhattan real estate was in a slump, and banks were wary of lending money for risky ventures, particularly ones involving rundown properties like the Commodore. But Donald wasn't discouraged. He understood that the key to securing financing was to reduce the perceived risk of the project, and he knew exactly how to do it: by securing a tax abatement from the city.

At the time, New York City was desperate for investment. The city was on the verge of bankruptcy, and its leaders were eager to revitalize the local economy. Donald approached city officials with a bold proposal: in exchange for redeveloping the Commodore and turning it into a first-class hotel that would generate jobs and tax revenue, he wanted a tax abatement that would dramatically lower the hotel's property taxes for the first 40 years of operation. The city, eager for any sign of economic revitalization, agreed to the deal.

This tax abatement was a game-changer. By significantly lowering the hotel's future tax burden, Donald was able to secure the financing he needed from banks. It also demonstrated Donald's savvy in understanding how to leverage government incentives to make his projects financially viable. While other developers may have balked at the challenges of reviving a decaying hotel in a struggling city, Donald had found a way to make the numbers work. With financing in place and Hyatt as a partner, the Commodore Hotel project was officially underway.

But the work was just beginning. Donald's vision for the Commodore was not just to restore the hotel to its former glory, but to transform it into something entirely new—a modern, luxury hotel that would stand out in the crowded Manhattan market. He hired the architectural firm Gruzen & Partners to redesign the building, with a focus on creating a sleek, modern exterior that would reflect the transformation happening inside. The hotel's old brick façade was replaced with a shimmering glass curtain wall, giving it a striking, contemporary look that was unlike anything else in the area.

Inside, the hotel underwent a complete gut renovation. Every aspect of the Commodore was redesigned and upgraded to meet Donald's high standards of luxury. The once-faded interiors were replaced with elegant, modern furnishings, and the hotel's public spaces were designed to impress, with marble floors, high-end finishes, and dramatic lighting. Donald's attention to detail was evident in every aspect of the renovation, from the opulent lobby to the finely crafted guest rooms. His goal was clear: to create a hotel that would not only attract business travelers but also symbolize the rebirth of New York City's hotel industry.

The grand reopening of the Commodore in 1980, now branded as the Grand Hyatt New York, was a triumph. The hotel quickly became one of the most popular in the city, attracting both tourists and business travelers with its prime location and luxurious amenities. It was the first new hotel to open in Manhattan in many years, and its success marked the beginning of a larger trend of revitalization in the city's real estate market. For Donald, the Grand Hyatt wasn't just a financial success—it was proof that he had what it took to succeed in Manhattan.

The Commodore Hotel deal was more than just a real estate project; it was a statement. Donald had taken a failing property, secured the necessary partnerships and financing, and turned it into a success story that revitalized a key part of Manhattan. The deal showcased his ability to think creatively, negotiate aggressively, and execute a complex project in a challenging environment. More importantly, it gave him the credibility he needed to be taken seriously by Manhattan's elite. With the success of the Grand Hyatt, Donald Trump was no longer an outsider looking in—he had officially arrived as a force to be reckoned with in the world of New York real estate.

Leveraging the Media to Build His Brand

The success of the Commodore Hotel deal was not just a real estate victory for Donald Trump; it was also a media triumph. From early in his career, Donald recognized the importance of the media in shaping public perception, and he was a master at using it to his advantage. The transformation of the crumbling Commodore into the gleaming Grand Hyatt New York provided him with the perfect opportunity to position himself as more than just a real estate developer—it allowed him to craft a public image as a visionary businessman and a bold risk-taker. Donald understood that success in Manhattan wasn't just about making deals; it was about being seen, talked about, and ultimately, becoming a household name.

Donald's ability to court media attention became one of his most potent tools in building the Trump brand. He knew that if he could keep his name in the headlines, it would amplify his achievements and create a perception of continuous success, even when the details were more nuanced. In the late 1970s and early 1980s, New York City was still grappling with financial and social crises, and the public craved stories of resurgence and ambition. Donald capitalized on this by framing himself as the young developer who was breathing new life into the city. The story of the Commodore's rebirth became a symbol of New York's comeback, and Donald positioned himself as the driving force behind it.

While many real estate developers shied away from the limelight, preferring to work quietly behind the scenes, Donald embraced the attention. He understood that in the competitive Manhattan market, being visible could be as important as the deals themselves. Media attention not only enhanced his reputation but also made it easier for him to attract investors, tenants, and partners. The more his name appeared in newspapers and magazines, the more people wanted to be associated with him. Whether through articles in *The New York Times*, interviews with local television stations, or appearances at high-profile events, Donald made sure that his presence in Manhattan was not just physical—it was also psychological.

One of the ways Donald skillfully engaged the media was by feeding them a constant stream of stories that showcased his larger-than-life personality and ambitions. He gave interviews where he emphasized the scale and significance of his projects, often using hyperbole to create excitement around his developments. He portrayed the Grand Hyatt as not just a hotel renovation but as a symbol of something greater—the revitalization of a city that had been down on its luck. His personal narrative became intertwined with New York's own story of resurgence, and the media was more than happy to tell it.

Donald also understood the value of controlling his image. Rather than waiting for the media to come to him, he often proactively reached out to journalists, ensuring that they had access to his latest projects and business moves. He famously employed his own press team to manage his public relations, including sending out press releases under different pseudonyms to draw attention to himself. This clever manipulation of the media helped ensure that Donald was always portrayed as the dynamic, young mogul reshaping the city's skyline.

His relationship with the tabloids, particularly *The New York Post* and *The Daily News*, was especially crucial. Donald realized that while highbrow publications like *The New York Times* were important for credibility, it was the tabloids that could help him connect with a broader audience. These publications had a massive readership, and their focus on sensational headlines made them perfect platforms for Donald's brand of self-promotion. He became a fixture in their pages, with stories about his latest deals, his luxurious lifestyle, and his ambitious plans for the future. The tabloids loved Donald's mix of boldness, glamour, and controversy, and he gave them plenty to write about.

In many ways, Donald's media strategy was ahead of its time. He recognized that in an age of increasing mass media consumption, a public persona could be as valuable as the physical assets he owned. He wasn't just building skyscrapers; he was building a brand—one that was inextricably linked to his name. The Trump name soon became synonymous with luxury, ambition, and success. It wasn't just the hotels or buildings that bore his name that mattered; it was the idea of *Trump* itself. Donald wasn't just selling real estate; he was selling an image, a lifestyle, and a sense of aspiration.

This media presence also served another critical function: it made Donald's projects seem bigger and more important than they might have appeared on paper. The constant media coverage helped to create an aura of inevitability around his success. Potential investors, partners, and even competitors began to see Donald as a rising star, someone who was always on the verge of his next big deal. This perception made it easier for Donald to secure financing, strike deals, and attract attention to future ventures. The narrative of success often became a self-fulfilling prophecy, as media coverage helped legitimize his ambitions.

Donald's ability to manipulate the media extended beyond traditional outlets. He cultivated an image as a socialite and public figure, often attending charity galas, fundraisers, and high-profile events, where he would rub shoulders with celebrities, politicians, and other influential figures. His public appearances were carefully orchestrated to reinforce his persona as a charismatic and powerful figure, one who could move seamlessly between the world of high finance and the world of celebrity. By making himself a fixture in New York's social scene, Donald ensured that his name was always in the conversation, both in business and in popular culture.

Perhaps most impressively, Donald understood the value of controversy. He recognized that not all media coverage needed to be positive to be beneficial. In fact, the more polarizing he became, the more attention he attracted. Whether he was clashing with city officials, sparring with critics, or making bold claims about his future projects, Donald ensured that his name was always at the center of the conversation. He thrived on the tension between admiration and skepticism, knowing that as long as people were talking about him, he was winning.

By the time the Grand Hyatt opened in 1980, Donald Trump had done more than just renovate a hotel—he had established himself as a media sensation. His ability to command headlines and shape his public image turned him into one of the most recognizable names in New York. The Commodore deal had been a bold gamble, but Donald's media savvy ensured that its success resonated far beyond the world of real estate. He had transformed himself into a brand, and that brand would soon become his most valuable asset. The Trump name was no longer just a family legacy from Queens—it was a symbol of ambition, luxury, and power on the global stage.

The Birth of the Trump Brand

By the time the Grand Hyatt opened its doors in 1980, Donald Trump had not only completed a successful real estate project but had also laid the foundation for something far more lasting: the Trump brand. The Commodore Hotel deal marked a pivotal moment in his career, transforming him from a local real estate developer into a figure of national prominence. Donald wasn't content with merely building hotels or office towers; he was intent on building a name—one that stood for luxury, success, and a kind of bold ambition that captured the public imagination. The Trump brand would soon become synonymous with high-end real estate and, eventually, a global lifestyle empire.

From the outset, Donald understood the power of branding, even if he wasn't using the term as explicitly back then. For him, the name "Trump" was more than just a signature at the bottom of contracts—it was a symbol of his identity, vision, and the standard of excellence he wanted to project. Unlike many real estate developers who worked quietly in the background, content to let their buildings speak for themselves, Donald wanted every project to carry his personal stamp. He realized that by associating his name with his developments, he could create a halo effect, making both the properties and himself more valuable.

The Grand Hyatt project gave him his first significant opportunity to begin branding himself in this way. Although the hotel was owned and operated in partnership with Hyatt, Donald ensured that his involvement was highly visible. His name might not have been on the hotel's marquee, but it was in every news article, every interview, and every press release. It was clear to the public that the transformation of the Commodore into the Grand Hyatt was a "Trump deal," and that association added an aura of prestige and accomplishment to the project. More importantly, it set the stage for what would become the defining strategy of his career: using his name as a symbol of quality and success.

For Donald, branding wasn't just about ego—it was a strategic business move. He recognized that the real estate market was incredibly competitive, and that a well-crafted image could set him apart from the pack. By positioning himself as a visionary developer who could turn around failing properties and bring glamour back to Manhattan, Donald created a perception of reliability and success. Investors wanted to be part of his projects because they believed in the power of the Trump name. Tenants and buyers flocked to his properties because they associated them with luxury and prestige. The brand became a selling point in itself, an asset that had real financial value.

As Donald's career progressed, this branding strategy would only intensify. He began to insist that his name be prominently displayed on his projects, starting with the iconic Trump Tower, which would open in 1983. This building would become the ultimate symbol of the Trump brand, with his name emblazoned in large gold letters on the façade. Trump Tower wasn't just a real estate development—it was a physical embodiment of everything Donald wanted his name to represent: wealth, power, and success.

It became a landmark not only because of its prime location on Fifth Avenue but because it was inseparable from the public persona Donald had crafted for himself.

Donald's use of his name as a brand wasn't limited to real estate. He quickly realized that the Trump name had value far beyond the properties he was developing. As his fame grew, so did the demand for his name to be associated with a wide range of ventures. He began licensing the Trump brand to everything from luxury goods to hotels, casinos, and even television shows. His brand became an entity unto itself, capable of generating revenue and recognition without him having to invest directly in the underlying business. This was an unprecedented move in the real estate world, where developers typically focused on bricks and mortar, not marketing themselves as global icons.

What set Donald apart was his understanding that in the modern world, a name could be as powerful as any physical asset. He treated his name as intellectual property, recognizing that it carried with it a certain cachet that could drive consumer behavior. People wanted to stay in a "Trump" hotel, live in a "Trump" apartment, or work in a "Trump" office building because it made them feel successful by association. The brand wasn't just about Donald Trump's personal achievements—it was about the aspiration of everyone who interacted with his properties and products.

The emergence of the Trump brand also signaled a shift in how Donald approached business. No longer content to be just a real estate developer, he began to see himself as a global entrepreneur, capable of leveraging his name into multiple industries. In time, the Trump Organization would expand into hospitality, entertainment, and even education, with the creation of ventures like Trump Hotels, Trump Golf, and Trump University. Each of these enterprises was designed to capitalize on the strength of the

Trump name, using it as a shorthand for luxury, exclusivity, and high standards.

Of course, branding also carried its risks, and Donald was well aware of that. By putting his name on everything he touched, he ran the risk of overextending or damaging the brand if any of his ventures failed. But for Donald, the potential rewards outweighed the risks. He believed that his relentless pursuit of success and his ability to generate media attention would ensure that the Trump brand remained strong, regardless of the challenges he faced. This confidence in his ability to control the narrative was a hallmark of his career, and it allowed him to weather setbacks that might have derailed other developers.

Ultimately, the creation of the Trump brand was about more than just business—it was about legacy. Donald wanted his name to endure long after he was gone, and he saw the Trump brand as a way to achieve that. By building an empire that was inseparable from his identity, he ensured that his influence would stretch far beyond any individual project or business deal. The Trump name had become larger than life, representing not just a man, but a vision of success that transcended borders and industries.

The Commodore Hotel deal may have been the catalyst for Donald's rise in Manhattan, but its most lasting impact was the birth of the Trump brand. What started as a calculated effort to break into New York's elite real estate scene had evolved into something far greater—a global brand that would come to symbolize ambition, luxury, and success for decades to come. With the Trump name now firmly established in the public consciousness, Donald was ready to take his empire to new heights, and the world would soon see just how far the Trump brand could reach.

| 3 |

Chapter 3: Trump Tower and Brand Expansion

The Vision for Trump Tower

In the late 1970s, as Donald Trump's reputation as a rising real estate developer solidified, he set his sights on an audacious project that would change not only his career trajectory but the skyline of Manhattan itself: Trump Tower. While Donald had already made headlines with his successful renovation of the Commodore Hotel into the Grand Hyatt, he knew that if he was to become a dominant figure in New York City's cutthroat real estate scene, he needed to create something extraordinary—something iconic. The vision for Trump Tower was born out of his desire to build more than just a building; he wanted to create a symbol of modern luxury and opulence that would bear his name and redefine Fifth Avenue.

The site for Trump Tower was crucial to his vision. It wasn't just about putting up a tall building—it was about location, prestige, and making a statement. Fifth Avenue, long the heart of Manhattan's most exclusive shopping and real estate district, was the ideal setting. In 1979, Donald secured the rights to the Bonwit Teller building, an aging department store with a prime location between 56th and 57th streets. It was here that he saw the potential for something grand, a skyscraper that would attract the world's elite and stand out as a monument to his ambition.

Securing the site was no simple task. The Bonwit Teller building had its own history, and demolishing it to make way for Trump Tower would require a complicated series of negotiations. But Donald was nothing if not persistent. He recognized that this location would give him the visibility he needed to transform himself from a developer into a brand. As he saw it, Fifth Avenue was where the city's most powerful people worked, shopped, and lived, and his tower would be at the center of it all.

The vision Donald had for Trump Tower extended beyond simply being another high-rise in a city full of skyscrapers. He wanted it to be a place that embodied luxury at every level—an address that conveyed success, wealth, and influence. From the beginning, Donald knew that the tower would cater to New York's wealthy elite, and he planned to create a mixed-use space that included not only luxurious residential condos but also high-end commercial and retail spaces. It wasn't enough for him to fill the building with tenants; he wanted to fill it with the most exclusive brands and the wealthiest buyers. He dreamed of creating a building where celebrities, moguls, and dignitaries would want to live and work, thereby turning Trump Tower into an icon of success.

To make this vision a reality, Donald needed more than just prime real estate—he needed to ensure the tower stood out architecturally. It was during this time that he hired the architect Der Scutt to bring his ideas to life. Scutt was a modernist known for his bold designs, and together, they conceived of a building that would be as striking visually as it was luxurious. One of Donald's key demands was that the tower's façade be made entirely of reflective glass and bronze, creating a sleek, modern exterior that would shine in the sunlight and give the building a distinct, high-end appearance. The shimmering, reflective surfaces would signal wealth and power to all who passed by, ensuring that Trump Tower wasn't just another addition to the skyline but a statement of prestige.

But Donald's vision didn't stop at the façade. He knew that the interior of the building had to be just as awe-inspiring as the exterior. He envisioned a grand, open atrium with a waterfall cascading down a massive wall of polished marble, complete with luxury retail stores, restaurants, and lavish common areas that would impress even the most jaded New Yorkers. Trump Tower wasn't just going to be a place to live or work—it was going to be an experience, a destination in its own right. The opulence of the building's design was central to Donald's strategy: anyone who walked through its doors would immediately feel they were in a world of luxury, and that feeling would be associated with the Trump name.

However, building a 58-story skyscraper in the heart of Manhattan came with its share of logistical and financial challenges. One of the most significant hurdles Donald faced was acquiring the necessary air rights to build as high as he wanted. At the time, New York City had strict zoning regulations that limited the height of new buildings. To get around this, Donald negotiated a deal with Tiffany & Co., whose flagship store was next door, to purchase their unused air rights. This allowed him to increase the height of Trump Tower, giving it the impressive stature that became a key part of its allure. The deal with Tiffany wasn't just practical—it was symbolic. Being able to build higher than the competition fit with Donald's overall vision of always reaching for more, always aiming to outdo those around him.

Donald's vision for Trump Tower also extended to the people who would inhabit the building. He didn't just want any tenants—he wanted the rich, the famous, and the influential. From the outset, his goal was to sell the residential units to celebrities, top executives, and foreign dignitaries who would add prestige to the building. The luxury retail spaces on the ground floors were similarly designed to attract only the most exclusive brands. Trump Tower wasn't just real estate; it was a status symbol, and Donald knew that the success of the project hinged on cultivating that image.

By the time Trump Tower opened its doors in 1983, it was clear that Donald Trump had achieved exactly what he had set out to do. The tower wasn't just another luxury building on Fifth Avenue—it was a statement of power, wealth, and success. More importantly, it was a tangible embodiment of Donald Trump's personal brand, one that would carry him forward into even larger ventures. Trump Tower had become more than just a real estate project; it was a symbol of what was to come—the birth of the Trump brand as a global phenomenon.

The Design and Construction of Trump Tower

The design and construction of Trump Tower were as ambitious and bold as Donald Trump's vision for the building itself. From the outset, Donald knew that this tower had to be more than just functional—it needed to be a spectacle, an architectural marvel that would turn heads and elevate his name in the world of high-end real estate. Every decision, from the materials used in the façade to the interior layout, was carefully crafted to convey a sense of luxury, grandeur, and modern sophistication.

To bring his vision to life, Donald enlisted architect Der Scutt, a renowned modernist whose previous works included high-profile buildings like One Astor Plaza and the U.N. Plaza Hotel. Scutt's sleek, modern style aligned with Donald's desire to create a building that would stand out in a city filled with skyscrapers. Together, they designed a 58-story glass-and-steel tower that would rise above Fifth Avenue, a gleaming beacon of wealth and power in the heart of Manhattan.

One of the most distinctive features of Trump Tower's design was its use of reflective glass and bronze finishes on the exterior. While many buildings of the era were constructed with concrete or brick, Donald wanted something that would shimmer in the sunlight, creating a sleek, contemporary look that projected both opulence and modernity. The bronze-tinted glass not only gave the building a unique visual identity but also symbolized the luxury that Donald wanted to be synonymous with the Trump name. As sunlight hit the tower during different times of the day, the reflective surfaces would glow in various shades of gold and bronze, making the building appear almost like a jewel amidst the concrete jungle of New York City.

The design wasn't just about aesthetics; it was about making a statement. Trump Tower's reflective exterior was a visual metaphor for Donald Trump's approach to business and life: bold, confident, and unapologetically extravagant. This gleaming tower wasn't merely a building—it was a monument to ambition, a visible declaration of Donald's intent to dominate the world of high-end real estate.

But the tower's design wasn't only about what was on the outside. The interior was equally as impressive and, in many ways, even more important to Donald's vision of luxury. The centerpiece of Trump Tower's interior was its grand atrium, a five-story open space that featured a massive indoor waterfall cascading down a marble wall. The waterfall, made of pink Breccia Pernice marble imported from Italy, flowed down into a pool surrounded by lush greenery, giving the space a sense of calm and grandeur. It wasn't just a decorative feature—it was a statement of elegance and extravagance that immediately conveyed the luxury experience that residents, shoppers, and visitors would expect inside the tower.

The atrium was lined with high-end retail shops, restaurants, and cafes, ensuring that anyone who entered Trump Tower would be immersed in a world of luxury from the moment they walked through the doors. Donald had a very clear vision: Trump Tower wouldn't just be a building—it would be a destination. People would come not only to live or work but also to experience the luxury lifestyle that the Trump name promised. The retail space was reserved for only the most exclusive brands, adding to the allure of the building. By attracting world-class retailers, Donald ensured that the Trump Tower address would become synonymous with wealth and prestige.

The use of marble didn't stop at the waterfall. Nearly every surface in the public areas of Trump Tower was covered in polished marble, creating an atmosphere of opulence that was unmatched in most of New York's high-end developments. Pink, cream, and black marble lined the floors, walls, and staircases of the building, reflecting light and adding to the overall sense of grandeur. Every detail, from the gold-accented elevator doors to the bronze handrails, was meticulously designed to enhance the feeling of wealth and exclusivity.

Of course, building something this extravagant in the heart of Manhattan was no small feat. The construction of Trump Tower was a massive undertaking, involving a complex series of negotiations, zoning challenges, and engineering feats. One of the first hurdles Donald had to overcome was the demolition of the existing Bonwit Teller building, an iconic department store that had stood on the site for decades. The building's art deco façade was historically significant, and the demolition sparked controversy when some of the decorative sculptures that adorned the building were destroyed instead of being preserved as promised. While this caused a public relations challenge, Donald remained focused on the bigger picture—constructing his tower as quickly and efficiently as possible to ensure its success.

Zoning restrictions presented another significant obstacle. Donald's vision for Trump Tower was ambitious, and in order to achieve the height and scale he wanted, he needed to negotiate with city officials to secure additional air rights. He struck a deal with Tiffany & Co., whose flagship store sat adjacent to the Trump Tower site, to purchase their unused air rights. This allowed Trump Tower to soar higher than the surrounding buildings, giving it a commanding presence on the skyline and cementing its status as a landmark on Fifth Avenue. The air rights deal wasn't just about adding height; it was about ensuring that Trump Tower would stand out, making it a more desirable address for the wealthy and powerful.

The construction itself posed numerous engineering challenges. Trump Tower's mixed-use nature—housing retail, office space, and luxury condos—required innovative solutions to maximize space and create a seamless flow between different areas of the building. The residential units, located on the upper floors, offered sweeping views of Central Park and the Manhattan skyline, making them some of the most sought-after properties in the city. The lower floors were reserved for commercial and retail use, while the middle floors contained office spaces, ensuring that Trump Tower catered to a diverse range of high-end clientele.

Despite the challenges, the construction of Trump Tower moved forward at an impressive pace. Donald was heavily involved in every aspect of the project, from selecting materials to overseeing the layout of the building's public spaces. He ensured that no expense was spared in creating a building that would reflect his vision of luxury and success. Trump Tower wasn't just a business venture—it was a personal statement about who Donald Trump was and what he stood for. The building would be his legacy, a symbol of his ambition and his belief that luxury, success, and the Trump name were inextricably linked.

By the time Trump Tower was completed in 1983, it was clear that Donald had succeeded in creating something extraordinary. The building stood as a gleaming symbol of wealth and ambition, with its distinctive glass façade and opulent interior drawing the attention of New Yorkers and visitors alike. It wasn't just a building—it was a brand, and it would serve as the cornerstone of Donald Trump's future business ventures, establishing him as one of the most recognizable names in real estate. With Trump Tower, Donald had not only changed the landscape of Manhattan—he had cemented his own place in the world of luxury real estate.

Trump Tower's Impact on New York and Donald's Image

When Trump Tower opened its doors in 1983, it wasn't just the culmination of a grand real estate project—it was the beginning of a transformation in how both Donald Trump and New York City were perceived. The tower stood tall as a symbol of a new era in Manhattan real estate, combining luxury, ambition, and celebrity appeal. In the process, it elevated Donald Trump from an ambitious developer to a cultural icon. Trump Tower quickly became more than just a building; it was a beacon of power and success, reshaping Fifth Avenue and redefining luxury living in the city.

From the moment the doors swung open, Trump Tower garnered intense media attention. Its prime location on Fifth Avenue, the opulent design, and Donald Trump's relentless self-promotion made the building an instant sensation. Newspapers and magazines ran stories not just about the tower's stunning design but about Donald himself, positioning him as a new kind of real estate tycoon—flashy, confident, and unafraid to make bold moves.

Trump Tower was described as "unapologetically lavish," a building that embraced extravagance at every turn, from the marble-clad atrium to the glittering glass exterior. Donald's vision had paid off: he had created a spectacle that the city couldn't stop talking about.

What made Trump Tower stand out wasn't just its height or its design; it was the way Donald Trump marketed it. He understood the value of creating a brand around the building, making sure that the Trump name was associated with luxury, wealth, and exclusivity. The apartments in Trump Tower were priced at a premium, far higher than similar properties in Manhattan, but that was part of the appeal. Owning a piece of Trump Tower wasn't just about buying real estate—it was about buying into the Trump brand. Donald's sales pitch wasn't just about square footage or views; it was about status. He positioned Trump Tower as the ultimate address for the world's elite.

In a stroke of marketing genius, Donald made sure that the building's early buyers were high-profile individuals who would enhance its prestige. From celebrities to foreign dignitaries, the list of Trump Tower's residents read like a who's who of the global elite. One of the first buyers was actor Bruce Willis, whose purchase made headlines and signaled to others that Trump Tower was where the rich and famous lived. Other notable residents included Andrew Lloyd Webber, Johnny Carson, and later, pop icon Michael Jackson. This strategy of filling the tower with celebrities added to its allure, making it a sought-after address for anyone looking to be part of New York's elite social scene.

But Trump Tower didn't just change the real estate landscape—it had a profound impact on Donald Trump's personal brand. Before the tower's completion, Donald was known as a successful real estate developer, but his name hadn't yet become the cultural touchstone it would eventually be. Trump Tower changed that. As the building rose to prominence, so did Donald's public profile. He wasn't just a developer; he was now a brand in his own right, someone whose name evoked images of luxury, power, and success. Donald quickly became a regular on the New York social circuit, rubbing elbows with the city's most influential figures, from politicians to media moguls. He was frequently featured in gossip columns and business magazines, and his name began to be mentioned alongside other New York power players like David Rockefeller and Rupert Murdoch.

The success of Trump Tower also catapulted Donald onto the national and international stage. News outlets from around the world covered the tower's opening, and Donald was more than happy to give interviews, appearing on television and in print to talk not just about the building, but about his vision for the future. His personality—larger-than-life, self-assured, and unrelenting—captivated audiences. Trump Tower wasn't just a building in New York; it became a symbol of American ambition and excess, and Donald was its poster child.

The impact of Trump Tower on Fifth Avenue and Manhattan's real estate market was undeniable. Before the tower, luxury developments in the city were mostly confined to pre-war buildings on the Upper East Side. Fifth Avenue, while prestigious, was better known for its shopping than for high-end residential real estate. Trump Tower changed that. Its presence on Fifth Avenue, just blocks away from Central Park, redefined the street as a luxury address, sparking a wave of high-end developments in the area. Other developers quickly followed Donald's lead, and within a few years, Fifth Avenue had transformed into one of the most coveted residential locations in the city. Trump Tower had set a new standard for luxury living, one that would influence real estate trends for decades.

Beyond its impact on the real estate market, Trump Tower became a cultural landmark. It wasn't just a place where people lived or worked—it was a destination. The building's atrium, with its waterfall, marble floors, and luxury shops, attracted visitors from all over the world. Tourists flocked to Trump Tower to experience its opulence, to shop in its high-end stores, and, if they were lucky, to catch a glimpse of Donald Trump himself. It was not uncommon to see Donald walking through the atrium, greeting visitors or conducting media interviews, always careful to keep himself—and his building—in the spotlight.

The building also became a backdrop for popular culture. Trump Tower appeared in movies, television shows, and commercials, further embedding it in the public consciousness. It was more than a building; it was a symbol of success and the aspirational lifestyle that so many sought. Trump Tower wasn't just where the rich lived—it was where people wanted to be seen.

As Trump Tower's fame grew, so did Donald's influence. The tower gave him the financial success and the public visibility he needed to expand his empire beyond real estate. With the success of Trump Tower, Donald Trump had established himself not just as a developer, but as a brand, one that transcended real estate and entered the worlds of media, entertainment, and politics. The tower had solidified his reputation as a man who could turn vision into reality, and it would serve as the foundation for the many ventures—both successful and risky—that would come in the years to follow.

Trump Tower was more than just another development project; it was a turning point in Donald Trump's career. It redefined what a luxury building could be, reshaped the Manhattan real estate market, and propelled Donald into the public eye in ways he had never experienced before. By building Trump Tower, Donald Trump had not only transformed Fifth Avenue—he had transformed himself into a global figure whose name would become synonymous with success.

The Role of Celebrity and Media in Building the Trump Brand

Donald Trump understood early on that success in real estate was not just about building impressive structures—it was also about building a public persona. With Trump Tower, he didn't just create a physical symbol of luxury; he leveraged its visibility to cultivate his image as the ultimate businessman. One of the key strategies Donald employed in promoting Trump Tower—and by extension, himself—was his mastery of media and celebrity culture. This was not merely a luxury residential and commercial skyscraper; it was the stage for Donald's transformation from developer to international celebrity.

As the tower was nearing completion, Donald began what would become a lifelong habit: using the media to promote his ventures, enhance his personal brand, and control the narrative around his projects. Rather than rely solely on traditional real estate marketing, he brought Trump Tower into the public eye through high-profile events, celebrity partnerships, and relentless media coverage. Every step of the construction, every key decision, and every major deal was an opportunity for publicity, and Donald made sure that the press was always aware of the progress.

Donald's innate understanding of the power of media allowed him to turn the unveiling of Trump Tower into a cultural event. He invited journalists, politicians, and celebrities to the building's grand opening, ensuring that it received widespread coverage. Major newspapers, magazines, and television networks covered the spectacle, with headlines not just praising the building's architectural grandeur but also focusing on Donald's growing status as a business leader. By making himself the face of Trump Tower, Donald created a direct association between the building and his personal brand. The tower wasn't just a place where the wealthy could live and shop—it was a reflection of Donald's ambitions and style. He made sure that when people talked about Trump Tower, they were also talking about Donald Trump.

One of the most important tactics Donald used to elevate Trump Tower's profile was to fill it with celebrities. He recognized that if high-profile individuals chose to live and work in Trump Tower, it would reinforce the building's status as the ultimate symbol of luxury and success. With his connections in the entertainment and sports industries, Donald was able to attract an impressive roster of celebrity tenants, many of whom were publicly associated with the building from the outset. The presence of stars such as Johnny Carson, Sophia Loren, and Andrew Lloyd Webber in the building's early days helped cement its reputation as a glamorous address, and Donald wasted no time in making sure that the media covered every new high-profile resident.

But it wasn't just the celebrities living in Trump Tower who contributed to its allure. Donald also courted the entertainment industry to feature the building in films, television shows, and commercials. The tower's opulent design and its location on Fifth Avenue made it a desirable backdrop for stories of wealth and power, and Donald was eager to allow filmmakers and TV producers to showcase the building. One of the most famous appearances of Trump Tower came in the movie *The Wolf of Wall Street*, where it served as a backdrop for scenes that symbolized financial success and excess. These appearances helped elevate Trump Tower from a New York City landmark to an internationally recognized symbol of the high life.

Donald's calculated use of media wasn't limited to traditional outlets, either. He knew that his public persona was just as important as the tower itself in attracting the right kind of attention. As a result, Donald carefully cultivated relationships with key journalists and media personalities, ensuring that stories about his success appeared regularly in print. He granted interviews to publications ranging from *The New York Times* to celebrity tabloids, discussing not only the tower's features but also his broader business philosophy. Donald's larger-than-life personality made him an engaging subject for the press, and he became a frequent guest on television programs, often discussing Trump Tower as a representation of his vision for success. Each media appearance reinforced the idea that Trump Tower, and by extension Donald Trump, was synonymous with luxury and achievement.

As his media presence grew, so did Donald's fame. He was no longer just a successful developer—he was a celebrity in his own right. By the mid-1980s, Donald Trump had become a household name, known not just for his real estate ventures but for his appearances on talk shows, in gossip columns, and at high-profile events. His ability to command media attention extended beyond the world of real estate and into popular culture. He made sure that every story about Trump Tower was also a story about him, and his carefully crafted image as a brash, confident, and unrelenting businessman made him one of the most talked-about figures in New York.

Of course, Donald's use of media wasn't just about promoting Trump Tower—it was about creating a personal brand that would transcend real estate. He understood that in the world of business, visibility was power. The more people knew his name, the more they associated it with success and luxury, and the easier it would be for him to expand into other ventures. Trump Tower was the foundation upon which Donald began to build a broader empire, one that would eventually include casinos, hotels, golf courses, and even his own television show.

But at the heart of all this was Donald's ability to create a narrative around Trump Tower that resonated with both the public and the elite. The media painted him as a man who could turn vision into reality, a developer who wasn't afraid to dream big and make it happen. Trump Tower became a symbol of this narrative—proof that Donald could take on massive projects, overcome challenges, and emerge victorious.

Donald's use of celebrity culture and media coverage to promote Trump Tower was a masterclass in branding. By intertwining the building's success with his own rising star, he turned Trump Tower into more than just a real estate venture. It became a key part of the mythology of Donald Trump—the self-made mogul who could turn steel and glass into a beacon of power and success. Through his savvy manipulation of media and celebrity, Donald ensured that Trump Tower was not only a commercial triumph but also a cultural landmark that would keep his name in the spotlight for years to come.

Ultimately, Trump Tower's success was as much about perception as it was about reality. Donald Trump understood that in the high-stakes world of New York real estate, image mattered just as much as the bottom line. By aligning himself with celebrities, making the tower a fixture in popular culture, and keeping himself in the media spotlight, Donald created an enduring legacy that would extend far beyond the walls of Trump Tower. It wasn't just a building—it was the embodiment of the Trump brand.

Trump Tower as the Foundation of a Global Brand

By the time Trump Tower was fully operational, it had not only transformed Donald Trump's real estate career but had also laid the groundwork for a global brand that would soon extend far beyond New York City. Trump Tower was more than just a skyscraper; it was the cornerstone of the Trump empire, a symbol of luxury, power, and ambition that would serve as a template for Donald's future ventures in real estate, hospitality, and entertainment. In many ways, Trump Tower was the beginning of Donald Trump's journey from real estate developer to international business icon.

As Trump Tower gained recognition as one of the premier addresses in New York City, Donald began to recognize the power of his own name as a brand. He saw that the "Trump" name itself had become synonymous with success, opulence, and high-end living. Trump Tower had cemented the notion that "Trump" was not just a surname but a mark of quality. This realization would become crucial in shaping Donald's business strategy moving forward. From this point on, he understood that the Trump name could be licensed, marketed, and extended to new projects, industries, and locations around the world.

The success of Trump Tower demonstrated that Donald had the ability not only to develop high-end properties but also to create a brand identity that people craved. In an era when luxury was increasingly defined by brand recognition, Donald capitalized on the Trump Tower name to expand his portfolio and, more importantly, his public persona. Soon, his name appeared on everything from luxury hotels to golf courses, casinos, and even an airline. While Trump Tower was rooted in bricks and mortar, its real power lay in the brand that Donald had built around it. And that brand would soon expand well beyond New York's skyline.

The first major expansion of the Trump brand outside of New York came in the form of Trump Plaza, a luxury hotel and casino in Atlantic City, New Jersey. Completed in 1984, just a year after Trump Tower's grand opening, Trump Plaza took many of the lessons Donald had learned from his flagship skyscraper and applied them to the world of gaming and hospitality. Like Trump

Tower, Trump Plaza was designed to cater to the ultra-wealthy, with lavish décor, high-stakes gambling, and exclusive amenities. Donald used the same marketing playbook that had made Trump Tower a success—promoting the project with media buzz, celebrity appearances, and his own larger-than-life personality.

The Atlantic City venture was the beginning of Donald's move into the hospitality and entertainment sectors, industries where the Trump brand would come to thrive. Over the next few years, he built a string of successful casinos, hotels, and resorts, many of which bore the Trump name. His portfolio expanded rapidly, and each new project further established the Trump brand as a global symbol of luxury and excess. Properties like the Trump Taj Mahal, a casino in Atlantic City that was billed as the "eighth wonder of the world," solidified Donald's reputation as a master of spectacle and high-end development.

But Donald didn't stop there. He recognized that the Trump brand could extend beyond real estate and hospitality to become a lifestyle brand. In the 1990s and 2000s, he began licensing his name to a wide range of products and businesses. Trump-branded merchandise, from ties and cologne to steaks and bottled water, began appearing on store shelves, all carrying the same promise of success and luxury that Trump Tower had established. While some ventures were more successful than others, the expansion of the Trump brand into consumer goods showed that Donald's real genius lay in his ability to market himself and his name.

Trump Tower also played a pivotal role in launching Donald into the world of media and entertainment. The building's high-profile nature attracted the attention of television producers, and Donald was soon making guest appearances on talk shows and reality TV programs, where he presented himself as the epitome of success. His public image as the confident, no-nonsense billionaire who could transform any project into a success captivated audiences, and it wasn't long before Donald made the leap into television full-time. In 2004, he launched *The Apprentice*, a reality TV show where contestants competed for a job at one of his companies. The show became a massive hit, further cementing Donald's image as a master businessman and savvy dealmaker.

The Apprentice wasn't just a television show—it was an extension of the Trump brand. Each episode was set in Trump Tower, and Donald made sure that the building itself was featured prominently in the show's visuals. The lavish offices, gleaming gold accents, and sweeping views of Manhattan all served as a backdrop to the drama unfolding on-screen, reinforcing the idea that Trump Tower was the ultimate symbol of power and success. Millions of viewers tuned in each week, and the show's catchphrase, "You're fired," became part of the cultural lexicon. With *The Apprentice*, Donald had not only created a new revenue stream but also introduced his brand to an even wider audience. Trump Tower, once a symbol of his real estate ambitions, had now become a symbol of his media empire.

As the Trump brand grew, Donald expanded internationally, taking the lessons he had learned from Trump Tower and applying them to new markets around the globe. Trump-branded properties began to appear in cities like Chicago, Las Vegas, Toronto, and Dubai, all designed with the same attention to luxury and exclusivity that had made Trump Tower a success. These international developments further established Donald as a global businessman and solidified his reputation as a builder of luxury properties.

Throughout all of these expansions, Trump Tower remained the heart of Donald's empire. It was his headquarters, his home, and the ultimate representation of what the Trump brand stood for. Visitors to the building could still find Donald walking through its gleaming marble atrium, meeting with high-profile clients, or entertaining the press. In many ways, Trump Tower continued to symbolize the Trump brand even as his empire grew beyond New York. For Donald, the tower was not just a real estate project—it was the physical manifestation of his ambition, a monument to his success, and a reminder that with enough vision and determination, anything was possible.

By building Trump Tower, Donald Trump had created more than just a luxurious skyscraper. He had laid the foundation for a global brand that would define his career and influence industries far beyond real estate. The tower was the catalyst for his expansion into hospitality, entertainment, and consumer goods, and it played a key role in transforming Donald from a successful developer into a cultural icon. For Donald Trump, Trump Tower wasn't just a building—it was the beginning of an empire.

| 4 |

Chapter 4: Risk and Reward: The Atlantic City Casi

Entering the Casino Business

By the early 1980s, Donald Trump had already made a name for himself as a dominant force in New York real estate, but his ambitions extended far beyond the skyscrapers and penthouses of Manhattan. With a keen eye for lucrative opportunities, Trump set his sights on a new frontier: the casino industry. Atlantic City, New Jersey, had recently become a hotbed for gambling, thanks to the legalization of casinos in 1976, and Trump saw immense potential in the rapidly growing market. For him, casinos were more than just a profitable venture—they were a high-stakes game where the rewards could be massive, and the risks equally daunting.

At the time, Atlantic City was in the midst of a transformation. Once a fading seaside resort, the city was reinventing itself as a gambling mecca to rival Las Vegas. Casino operators from around the country flocked to Atlantic City, lured by the promise of a booming gambling industry on the East Coast. Trump recognized that this was a chance to diversify his business empire and take advantage of the city's explosive growth. More importantly, he saw that casinos offered something his New York projects didn't: the ability to generate enormous cash flow from gaming operations, hotels, and entertainment all under one roof.

Trump's decision to enter the casino business was driven by a combination of timing, opportunity, and a healthy appetite for risk. The early success of Atlantic City's casino industry made it an attractive prospect for developers, and Trump's connections in real estate, combined with his ability to secure financing, gave him a competitive edge. However, he wasn't content to simply join the fray—he wanted to dominate the market. His vision was grand, as always. He didn't just want to build casinos; he wanted to create the most luxurious, high-profile gambling destinations in Atlantic City, rivaling anything Las Vegas had to offer.

In 1982, Trump made his first major move by acquiring a prime piece of real estate on the Atlantic City Boardwalk. The location was perfect, strategically placed near other major casinos, and gave him a foothold in the city's rapidly expanding casino district. With the land secured, Trump set out to build his first casino, Trump Plaza. The Plaza was designed to be an upscale gambling destination, catering to wealthy tourists and high rollers. Trump's goal was clear: to outshine the competition with a property that oozed luxury and exclusivity.

From the beginning, Trump's entry into the casino business was marked by bold decisions and careful planning. He recognized that casinos were not just about gambling—they were about creating an experience. Trump Plaza would be more than just a place to gamble; it would be a world-class resort with high-end dining, entertainment, and luxury accommodations. Trump understood that in the casino business, the environment was just as important as the games, and he spared no expense in ensuring that the Plaza would offer a first-class experience to its visitors.

As Trump Plaza neared completion, Trump's enthusiasm for the casino industry grew. He realized that Atlantic City was not just a side venture—it had the potential to become a cornerstone of his empire. The market was still developing, and Trump saw opportunities to expand beyond a single property. His plan was to build an empire in Atlantic City, much as he had in New York, and he quickly set his sights on a second casino, which would become Trump Castle.

Entering the casino business also meant navigating the complex regulatory landscape of New Jersey's gaming industry. Casinos were heavily regulated, and Trump had to obtain a gaming license from the New Jersey Casino Control Commission. This process involved extensive background checks, financial scrutiny, and a rigorous vetting process. Trump's reputation as a successful real estate developer worked in his favor, and he was granted a license to operate his casino. However, Trump was not the type to wait idly for approvals. He used his time during the licensing process to further promote Trump Plaza, generating buzz about the upcoming property and solidifying his reputation as Atlantic City's next big player.

Trump's entry into Atlantic City was also marked by his ability to secure financing for these massive projects. At a time when the city was booming, banks were eager to lend to developers who had a proven track record of success. Trump used his connections in the financial world to obtain the capital needed to bring his casino vision to life. He had a knack for leveraging other people's money—one of the key principles of his business philosophy. By using loans and partnerships, Trump was able to take on large-scale projects with minimal personal risk, a strategy that would define much of his business career.

As construction on Trump Plaza progressed, it became clear that Trump was not just another developer looking to cash in on Atlantic City's gambling boom. He was playing the long game, investing in a market that he believed had enormous potential.

His vision for Atlantic City extended beyond a single casino—he wanted to create a brand that would dominate the city's skyline and attract visitors from around the world. The Trump name, already synonymous with luxury in New York, would soon become synonymous with gambling in Atlantic City.

In the end, Trump's decision to enter the casino business was a calculated risk, but one that aligned perfectly with his ambition and vision for growth. Atlantic City offered him the opportunity to diversify his business interests, expand his brand, and tap into a lucrative market. While the risks were significant—high competition, regulatory hurdles, and the ever-present possibility of financial overextension—Trump was confident that the rewards would outweigh the challenges. His foray into Atlantic City marked the beginning of a new chapter in his business career, one that would bring both great success and great challenges in the years to come.

Trump Plaza and Trump Castle

Donald Trump's first major casino project in Atlantic City, Trump Plaza, opened its doors in 1984. This marked the beginning of a new chapter for Trump, one in which he would make a significant impact on the casino industry. Trump Plaza, a joint venture with Harrah's Entertainment, was a towering presence on the Atlantic City Boardwalk, strategically located in the heart of the city's bustling casino district. It was designed to exude luxury, sophistication, and exclusivity—key elements of Trump's brand from the start.

Trump Plaza wasn't just another casino; it was a statement of intent. Trump knew that the competition in Atlantic City was fierce, with established casinos like Caesars and Bally's already drawing massive crowds. To stand out, Trump needed to create an environment that appealed to both the high-end clientele and the everyday gambler. The Plaza's design reflected this balance—luxurious enough to attract wealthy patrons, but accessible enough to welcome a wide range of customers.

The lobby of Trump Plaza was a prime example of this strategy. Gleaming marble floors, crystal chandeliers, and gold accents were carefully selected to create an atmosphere of opulence. At the same time, Trump ensured that the casino floor was packed with state-of-the-art slot machines and a wide variety of table games, offering something for everyone. His philosophy was simple: in the casino business, you needed to appeal to both the wealthy and the masses. By creating a high-end environment with broad appeal, Trump hoped to establish Trump Plaza as a premier destination in Atlantic City.

Trump Plaza's success was driven by more than just the glitzy design and prime location. Trump had a knack for generating buzz and making his properties a focal point of media attention. He was a master of promotion, and the opening of Trump Plaza was no exception. He held an extravagant opening ceremony, attended by celebrities, politicians, and media personalities, making sure that the event received maximum coverage. The press eagerly followed Trump's every move, and his ability to dominate headlines gave Trump Plaza an edge over the competition. In many ways, Trump's ability to market his properties and himself was just as important as the quality of the casino itself.

As Trump Plaza began to thrive, Donald set his sights on expanding his presence in Atlantic City. His second major acquisition was the former Hilton Hotel and Casino, which he rebranded as Trump Castle. Situated just outside the main casino strip, Trump Castle was another bold gamble. The property had struggled under its previous ownership, but Trump saw an opportunity to turn it around. With his usual flair, he took control of the project and immediately set out to overhaul the casino, giving it the

Trump treatment—lavish renovations, aggressive marketing, and a new image of luxury.

Trump Castle was unique in that it catered to a different demographic than Trump Plaza. While the Plaza was located on the busy Boardwalk and aimed to attract tourists and casual gamblers, Trump Castle was more of a destination for serious players and high rollers. Trump believed that the casino's off-Boardwalk location would help it stand out, offering a more exclusive experience for guests who wanted to avoid the crowded streets and noise of the main casino strip. He marketed Trump Castle as a resort where visitors could enjoy luxury accommodations, world-class dining, and exclusive gaming, all while escaping the hustle of the Boardwalk.

One of Trump's smartest moves was appointing his then-wife, Ivana Trump, as the president of Trump Castle. Ivana was already a successful businesswoman, and her attention to detail and personal touch made Trump Castle a unique offering in Atlantic City's crowded market. Under her leadership, Trump Castle quickly developed a reputation for elegance and class. Ivana oversaw many of the property's renovations and improvements, ensuring that the casino maintained the highest standards of service and luxury. Her involvement also helped boost the Trump brand, as the image of the glamorous couple working together to build a business empire captivated the media.

Despite the risks involved, Trump's aggressive expansion strategy began to pay off. Trump Plaza and Trump Castle both saw strong performance in the early years, as Atlantic City's casino industry continued to grow. Trump Plaza, with its high visibility and central location, attracted waves of tourists and gamblers, while Trump Castle carved out a niche as a more exclusive, high-end destination. Trump's hands-on approach, combined with his flair for showmanship, helped both properties stand out in a crowded market.

But Trump's success in Atlantic City wasn't just a matter of luxury and spectacle. He understood the importance of customer loyalty in the casino business, and he invested heavily in programs to reward his most loyal patrons. Trump Plaza, in particular, developed a strong base of repeat customers, thanks to its generous player rewards and high-quality service. Trump realized that the casino business was about building relationships, not just one-time transactions. This understanding helped him cultivate a loyal customer base that kept returning to Trump properties, even as the competition intensified.

Trump Plaza and Trump Castle also served as platforms for Trump to experiment with different aspects of the casino business. He realized that casinos weren't just about gambling—they were about creating a comprehensive entertainment experience. Trump introduced big-name entertainers to his properties, hosting concerts and shows that drew even more visitors. By blending luxury accommodations, top-tier gaming, and world-class entertainment, Trump's casinos offered an all-encompassing experience that set them apart from their competitors.

The early success of Trump Plaza and Trump Castle was a testament to Donald Trump's ability to take risks and make bold moves in a competitive industry. He had entered Atlantic City at a time when the market was growing rapidly, but he wasn't content with just being another player in the game. From the beginning, Trump aimed to dominate the city's casino industry, and his ability to combine luxury, entertainment, and relentless marketing helped him achieve that goal. However, as with many of Trump's ventures, the rapid expansion came with significant risks, and the challenges that lay ahead would test his resilience as a businessman.

The Trump Taj Mahal: A Bold Gamble

As Donald Trump expanded his casino empire in Atlantic City with Trump Plaza and Trump Castle, he wasn't content to stop there. His vision for the city went far beyond simply owning successful casinos—he wanted to build something monumental, something that would solidify his legacy as the king of Atlantic City. That vision culminated in his most ambitious project yet: the Trump Taj Mahal. Dubbed "the Eighth Wonder of the World," the Taj Mahal was designed to be the largest and most extravagant casino in the world, a symbol of Trump's ability to take risks on an unprecedented scale.

The story of the Trump Taj Mahal began in 1988 when Trump purchased the unfinished project from Resorts International, a company that had initially broken ground on the casino but ran into financial trouble before completing it. Trump, always opportunistic, saw the Taj Mahal as the ultimate trophy in his Atlantic City empire. With his characteristic flair for showmanship, Trump rebranded the project, promising that the casino would be unlike anything the world had ever seen. He envisioned a palatial casino, dripping in luxury and opulence, where no expense was spared.

From the outset, the Taj Mahal was a bold gamble. The sheer scale of the project was daunting. It was designed to be the largest casino in Atlantic City, with over 120,000 square feet of gaming space, more than 2,000 hotel rooms, and numerous high-end restaurants, bars, and entertainment venues. The cost of constructing the Taj Mahal soared to nearly $1 billion, making it the most expensive casino project in history at the time. Trump's decision to push forward with such a massive undertaking was both a testament to his ambition and a reflection of his confidence in his ability to outshine the competition.

Trump's approach to the Taj Mahal was simple: bigger is better. Every detail of the casino was designed to be grander and more luxurious than anything Atlantic City had ever seen. The architecture was inspired by the famed Taj Mahal in India, with intricate domes, towers, and lavish decor. Inside, the casino was a sensory overload of gold, chandeliers, and marble. Trump spared no expense in making the Taj Mahal the ultimate luxury destination. To him, the Taj Mahal wasn't just another casino; it was a symbol of his business prowess and his ability to dream bigger than anyone else in the industry.

The Taj Mahal's marketing campaign reflected this grandeur. Trump hyped the casino relentlessly, with promises of world-class entertainment, unparalleled luxury, and the highest rollers in the business flocking to its doors. He made sure the opening event was nothing short of spectacular. The grand opening in April 1990 was a star-studded affair, featuring fireworks, celebrities, and a ribbon-cutting ceremony that received extensive media coverage. In typical Trump fashion, he made sure the world knew that the Taj Mahal was the crown jewel of Atlantic City.

But beneath the glitz and glamour, the financial realities of building the Taj Mahal were far more precarious. To fund the project, Trump took on an enormous amount of debt. He financed the construction through high-interest junk bonds, a risky move that would eventually come back to haunt him. The interest rates on these bonds were exceptionally high, meaning that even as the Taj Mahal raked in profits, Trump would be saddled with substantial debt payments. Nevertheless, Trump was undeterred. He was confident that the success of the Taj Mahal would more than cover its costs, and he moved forward with his grand vision, even as the financial risks mounted.

Trump's gamble on the Taj Mahal wasn't just about money—it was about legacy. For Trump, the Taj Mahal was more than just a business venture; it was a personal achievement, a monument to his name. He saw the Taj Mahal as his chance to leave an indelible mark on Atlantic City and the casino industry. No one could build casinos the way Trump could, and the Taj Mahal was his proof. He envisioned it as the ultimate destination for high rollers, tourists, and celebrities alike, a place where people would come not just to gamble, but to experience the height of luxury.

The size and scale of the Taj Mahal also reflected Trump's larger-than-life persona. He was a master at creating a spectacle, and the Taj Mahal was the ultimate expression of that talent. Trump knew that in the casino business, appearances mattered. It wasn't just about having the best slot machines or table games—it was about creating an environment where people felt like they were part of something special. The Taj Mahal was designed to do just that. From the moment visitors walked through its doors, they were enveloped in an atmosphere of grandeur and excitement, and that was exactly what Trump wanted.

However, as the Taj Mahal prepared to open its doors, the financial strain was beginning to show. The casino industry in Atlantic City was becoming increasingly competitive, with new properties opening and existing casinos vying for a share of the market. While the Taj Mahal promised to draw huge crowds, Trump's massive debt load meant that the casino would need to generate enormous profits just to keep up with interest payments. Nevertheless, Trump remained optimistic. He believed that the Taj Mahal would become the crown jewel of Atlantic City, a testament to his ability to turn risk into reward.

As the opening day approached, Trump was at the height of his powers in Atlantic City. With Trump Plaza and Trump Castle already established as major players in the market, the Taj Mahal was set to elevate Trump's casino empire to new heights. But while Trump's public persona was one of confidence and bravado, the reality behind the scenes was far more uncertain. The success of the Taj Mahal was not guaranteed, and the high-stakes gamble that Trump had undertaken was about to be put to the test.

In the end, the Trump Taj Mahal was both a triumph and a cautionary tale. It was a symbol of Trump's vision and ambition, but it also reflected the dangers of overreaching in a highly competitive and volatile industry. The financial burden of the Taj Mahal would eventually lead to major challenges for Trump's Atlantic City empire, but in the moment, it stood as a glittering testament to his belief that no risk was too great if the reward was spectacular enough.

Financial Struggles and Bankruptcy

By the time the Trump Taj Mahal opened in April 1990, it was already one of the most talked-about casinos in the world. The lavish opening, the scale of the project, and Donald Trump's relentless self-promotion had captured the attention of the public and media alike. However, behind the glittering facade, serious financial problems were brewing. The same boldness that had driven Trump to build the Taj Mahal on such a grand scale had also led him to take on a staggering amount of debt, and as the casino opened its doors, the weight of that debt threatened to unravel Trump's Atlantic City empire.

The financing of the Trump Taj Mahal was one of the riskiest moves of Trump's career. To complete the project, Trump had issued $675 million in junk bonds—high-risk, high-yield debt securities that were popular in the 1980s. While these bonds provided the capital Trump needed to finish construction, they came with an enormous price: sky-high interest rates of around 14%. That meant that even if the Taj Mahal performed well, Trump would face crushing interest payments that would eat into any profits.

For Trump, the gamble was clear—if the Taj Mahal succeeded beyond expectations, it would generate enough revenue to cover the debt and more. If it faltered, however, the financial consequences would be dire.

At first, the Taj Mahal seemed poised for success. As the largest casino in the world at the time, it drew crowds of visitors eager to see the opulent new resort and try their luck at the gaming tables. The casino boasted over 4,000 slot machines, a vast array of table games, and an enormous poker room, along with high-end restaurants, luxury suites, and entertainment venues that attracted top-tier talent. Trump had delivered on his promise of grandeur, and the Taj Mahal quickly became a symbol of Atlantic City's ambition and potential.

But even with all the fanfare, the financial realities began to set in. Atlantic City's casino market was already highly competitive, and the opening of the Taj Mahal didn't occur in a vacuum. Other casinos in the city, including Trump's own Trump Plaza and Trump Castle, now faced increased competition for the same pool of visitors. Rather than drawing new customers to Atlantic City, the Taj Mahal often cannibalized business from Trump's other properties, spreading his empire thinner than ever before. The high operating costs of maintaining the Taj Mahal, coupled with the enormous debt load, created a financial strain that Trump could not ignore.

As the months passed, it became clear that the Taj Mahal was not generating the kind of revenue needed to keep up with its crushing debt payments. While the casino was popular, the profits were not enough to offset the enormous interest on the junk bonds. Trump found himself in a precarious position: he owned the most luxurious casino in Atlantic City, but the financial structure supporting it was unsustainable. The same bold vision that had led Trump to build the Taj Mahal now seemed like a dangerous overextension, threatening the stability of his entire Atlantic City operation.

By 1991, just a year after the grand opening, the financial pressures had become overwhelming. The Trump Organization was unable to meet its debt obligations, and Trump was forced to file for Chapter 11 bankruptcy protection for the Trump Taj Mahal. The bankruptcy was a major blow to Trump's reputation as a business mogul, especially given his high-profile promises of success. The Chapter 11 filing allowed Trump to restructure the debt, reducing the interest payments and giving him more time to repay the loans, but it also meant giving up some control of the casino to creditors.

The bankruptcy of the Trump Taj Mahal was not an isolated event—it signaled a broader crisis within Trump's Atlantic City empire. Trump Plaza and Trump Castle were also struggling under their own debt burdens, and the financial strain of maintaining multiple large-scale casinos in a competitive market had stretched Trump's resources to the limit. In a span of just a few years, Trump had gone from being Atlantic City's most ambitious developer to being its most overextended.

For Trump, the bankruptcy filings were a painful but necessary step to keep his empire afloat. He worked tirelessly to renegotiate the terms of his debt with creditors, often using his personal charm and business acumen to strike deals that allowed him to retain some control over his properties. While the bankruptcy was a humbling experience, it was also a demonstration of Trump's resilience. He was not willing to walk away from Atlantic City, even in the face of mounting financial losses. Instead, he fought to preserve what he had built, using every tool at his disposal to stay in the game.

One of the most significant consequences of the bankruptcy was the loss of equity in the Trump Taj Mahal. In exchange for reducing his debt load, Trump was forced to give up a significant portion of ownership in the casino to bondholders and creditors. While Trump remained the public face of the Taj Mahal, his control over the property was diminished, and the financial benefits of any future success would be shared with others. Nevertheless, Trump managed to maintain a key role in the casino's management, and he continued to market the Taj Mahal as one of Atlantic City's premier destinations.

The bankruptcy filings also revealed the risks inherent in Trump's business strategy. Throughout his career, Trump had been known for taking on large amounts of debt to finance his projects, relying on the expectation that future profits would more than cover the costs. In many cases, this strategy had worked, allowing Trump to build his empire with relatively little personal capital. But in the case of the Taj Mahal, the scale of the debt and the competitive pressures in Atlantic City proved too much to overcome.

Despite the financial setbacks, Trump continued to portray the Taj Mahal as a success. In public, he emphasized the grandeur and luxury of the casino, downplaying the financial difficulties behind the scenes. He pointed to the thousands of jobs the Taj Mahal had created and the economic impact it had on Atlantic City as evidence of its value. While the bankruptcy was a significant blow, Trump remained optimistic about the future of his Atlantic City empire.

In the end, the Trump Taj Mahal's bankruptcy was a turning point in Trump's business career. It exposed the risks of his high-leverage strategy, but it also demonstrated his ability to navigate financial crises and emerge with his brand intact. Trump's willingness to take risks had always been a defining feature of his business approach, and the Taj Mahal was no exception. The casino's financial struggles were a reminder that even the boldest visions can come with significant challenges, but for Trump, they were also a testament to the resilience that had defined his career.

Lessons Learned and the Legacy of Atlantic City

The Trump Taj Mahal's financial struggles and subsequent bankruptcy were a humbling moment for Donald Trump, but they were far from the end of his Atlantic City story. In fact, Trump saw these challenges as part of a broader learning experience, one that shaped his approach to business and risk management moving forward. Even though the Taj Mahal never fully realized its grand financial ambitions, the experience reinforced key lessons about leveraging assets, managing debt, and the importance of adaptability in the face of changing market conditions.

One of the most significant lessons Trump learned from the Taj Mahal was the danger of over-leveraging. Trump had always been comfortable using large amounts of debt to finance his projects, seeing it as a way to multiply his wealth without having to tie up too much personal capital. This strategy had worked well in the early years of his career, especially in real estate, where appreciating property values often allowed him to refinance or sell at a profit. However, the scale of the Taj Mahal project and the volatility of the casino industry exposed the risks of this approach. Trump came to realize that relying too heavily on debt could leave him vulnerable to market fluctuations and external pressures beyond his control.

After the Taj Mahal bankruptcy, Trump became more cautious in how he approached financing, focusing on building a stronger balance sheet and reducing his exposure to high-interest debt. This shift in strategy allowed him to weather future challenges with more stability, and it demonstrated his ability to learn from past mistakes without losing his appetite for ambitious projects.

In interviews and public statements, Trump often framed the Taj Mahal's financial troubles as part of the natural ebb and flow of business, emphasizing that any successful entrepreneur must be willing to take risks and face setbacks along the way.

The Trump Taj Mahal, despite its financial struggles, remained a symbol of Trump's grand vision and boldness. In the years following its bankruptcy, the casino continued to operate, albeit under a more conservative financial structure. Trump used the media attention surrounding the casino's ups and downs to keep his name and brand in the spotlight, always emphasizing the scale and luxury of the Taj Mahal, even as other properties in Atlantic City faltered. He understood that the Taj Mahal wasn't just a casino—it was a powerful marketing tool that reinforced his public persona as a dealmaker willing to push boundaries and take on monumental challenges.

For Trump, the experience in Atlantic City also highlighted the importance of branding. While the Taj Mahal, along with Trump Plaza and Trump Castle, faced financial difficulties, the Trump name continued to grow in prominence. Trump realized that his brand had value beyond the financial performance of any individual asset, and he began to focus more on leveraging his name as a key part of his business strategy. Whether the properties succeeded or struggled, they were always inextricably linked to Trump's persona, and this association helped him remain relevant in the business world, even in times of adversity.

The Atlantic City chapter of Trump's career also taught him valuable lessons about the casino industry itself. Casinos, unlike traditional real estate, were subject to intense competition and market saturation, as well as regulatory pressures that could change at any moment. Trump recognized that while casinos could be highly profitable, they were also fraught with risks, especially when the market became oversaturated as it did in Atlantic

City in the late 1980s and early 1990s. He came to understand that diversification across industries was essential for long-term success, and he began to explore other business opportunities, including his ventures into entertainment, branding, and later, reality television.

Trump's experience in Atlantic City also offered insights into the nature of risk-taking and its role in shaping his business philosophy. Throughout his career, Trump had always embraced risk, believing that the biggest rewards came to those who were willing to take bold actions. The Trump Taj Mahal was a perfect example of this philosophy—an audacious, billion-dollar bet on Atlantic City's future. While the financial outcome may not have been as successful as Trump had hoped, the experience reaffirmed his belief that risk and reward are inseparable in business. Trump's resilience in the face of setbacks was one of the defining characteristics of his career, and it was a trait that would serve him well in the years to come.

The legacy of Trump's Atlantic City empire is a complex one. On one hand, his casinos helped shape the city's identity during its heyday, drawing tourists, creating jobs, and providing a sense of excitement and opportunity. The Taj Mahal, in particular, stood as a towering symbol of what Atlantic City could aspire to be—a world-class gaming destination capable of attracting visitors from around the globe. Trump's relentless promotion of the city, his ability to generate buzz, and his sheer force of will played a significant role in elevating Atlantic City's profile during the 1980s and early 1990s.

On the other hand, Trump's Atlantic City ventures also serve as a cautionary tale about the risks of overexpansion and the challenges of sustaining large-scale projects in a competitive market. The financial struggles of the Taj Mahal, Plaza, and Castle mirrored the broader decline of Atlantic City itself, as the city struggled to compete with new gaming destinations like Las Vegas and regional casinos in neighboring states. While Trump remained a prominent figure in Atlantic City for many years, his eventual exit from the market reflected the changing dynamics of the casino industry and the limits of even the boldest business strategies.

In the years following the Taj Mahal bankruptcy, Trump would continue to evolve as a businessman, shifting his focus from casino ownership to other ventures, including real estate developments, television, and branding deals. The lessons he learned from Atlantic City—about risk, debt, and the power of branding—would inform his future decisions and shape his career as it moved in new directions. While the Taj Mahal and his other Atlantic City properties may no longer be part of Trump's empire, their legacy lives on as a testament to his ambition, resilience, and willingness to dream big.

In many ways, the Trump Taj Mahal and his broader Atlantic City experience encapsulate the essence of Donald Trump's business philosophy: to pursue bold visions, take calculated risks, and adapt to challenges along the way. For Trump, success was never just about financial results—it was about the brand, the spectacle, and the constant push to achieve something greater. And even when faced with setbacks, Trump's ability to turn adversity into opportunity ensured that his legacy in Atlantic City, and in business, would endure.

| 5 |

Chapter 5: The Art of the Deal

Trump's Business Philosophy

Donald Trump's rise to prominence in the business world was not just the result of his deal-making skills or his knack for identifying lucrative opportunities; it was also deeply rooted in a core philosophy that he carried throughout his career. In *The Art of the Deal*, Trump outlined the principles that guided him from his earliest ventures to his most ambitious projects. Central to this philosophy was the belief that thinking big, being passionate, and maintaining a clear vision were essential ingredients for success. These were not merely abstract concepts for Trump; they were actionable strategies that shaped his every decision.

From an early age, Trump was exposed to the world of real estate through his father, Fred Trump, a successful developer in Brooklyn and Queens. While Fred Trump operated in a relatively conservative, middle-income housing market, Donald was determined to make a name for himself on a much larger stage. He observed his father's attention to detail, his ability to manage construction projects, and his relentless focus on turning a profit, but Donald's aspirations went far beyond the neighborhoods where his father built affordable housing. He wanted to leave his mark on the skyline of Manhattan.

Trump's first principle, "Think Big," became one of the defining characteristics of his approach to business. He understood that
in order to stand out in the crowded and competitive world of
New York real estate, he needed to pursue projects that were not
only financially rewarding but also iconic. His ambition was evident in the types of deals he pursued—large-scale developments
that could capture public attention and reshape the city's landscape. For Trump, playing it safe was never an option. He believed
that success came to those who were willing to take bold risks,
push boundaries, and aim for projects that others might shy away
from. As he wrote in *The Art of the Deal*, "I like thinking big. I always have. To me, it's very simple: if you're going to be thinking
anyway, you might as well think big."

This mentality of thinking big translated into his projects like
the renovation of the Commodore Hotel into the Grand Hyatt,
the development of Trump Tower, and later his ventures into Atlantic City casinos. Trump understood that the scale and grandeur
of a project were often as important as the financials behind it. By
aiming high, he not only created profitable ventures but also built
his reputation as a larger-than-life figure in the business world.
These projects weren't just real estate developments; they were
statements of ambition and vision.

Another core aspect of Trump's philosophy was his unwavering passion for the work. Trump has often described himself as
someone who genuinely loves the thrill of making deals and creating something out of nothing. For him, business was not just
about the money—it was about the game. The process of negotiating, constructing, and transforming properties excited him. This
passion fueled his perseverance through challenges and setbacks.
Trump's enthusiasm for his projects was contagious, and it helped
him rally investors, attract media attention, and motivate teams to
deliver on his ambitious visions.

In *The Art of the Deal*, Trump also emphasized the importance of maintaining a clear vision. For Trump, this meant having a strong sense of direction and knowing exactly what he wanted to achieve from any given deal or project. Whether it was turning a rundown hotel into a luxury destination or transforming a barren stretch of Atlantic City into a casino empire, Trump always had a clear picture of what success looked like. This vision allowed him to stay focused, even in the face of obstacles. He was not easily swayed by external opinions or short-term setbacks because he remained fixated on the end goal.

Trump's vision was not just about the physical outcome of his projects but also about the way he positioned himself in the marketplace. He understood that creating a brand was as important as creating buildings. From early on, Trump's name was attached to his properties, and he made sure that name stood for luxury, success, and prestige. This focus on personal branding was a key element of his business philosophy and one that he would continue to leverage throughout his career. By associating his name with high-end developments, Trump ensured that every deal he made enhanced not just his financial portfolio but also his reputation.

Underpinning all of these principles was Trump's belief in resilience and adaptability. In business, as in life, setbacks are inevitable. Trump acknowledged that not every deal would go according to plan, and not every project would be an immediate success. However, he believed that the ability to pivot, renegotiate, and stay in the game was crucial to long-term success. This resilience, combined with his drive to think big and his passion for the work, helped him navigate some of the most challenging moments in his career.

Ultimately, Trump's business philosophy, as laid out in *The Art of the Deal*, was a reflection of his personality—bold, ambitious, and relentless. He believed that success wasn't just about having a good idea or a sound business plan; it was about having the courage to pursue that idea with everything you've got, even when the odds seem stacked against you. For Trump, business was not just a profession—it was a way of life, and his philosophy was the roadmap that guided him to build his empire.

Negotiation as a Key Skill

At the heart of Donald Trump's business success was his skill in negotiation, a talent he regarded as essential to deal-making and one he meticulously honed throughout his career. In *The Art of the Deal*, Trump described negotiation as both an art and a science, requiring instinct, strategy, and timing. His ability to secure favorable terms, navigate complex business relationships, and turn difficult situations to his advantage became the hallmark of his approach. Whether he was closing a multi-million-dollar real estate deal or brokering tax abatements with city officials, Trump's prowess in negotiation set him apart in a highly competitive industry.

One of Trump's core beliefs about negotiation was the importance of leverage. In every deal, he focused on finding a position of strength from which he could negotiate, and he did so with an acute awareness of the other party's needs and vulnerabilities. Trump understood that leverage wasn't just about having more money or better resources; it was about being in a position where the other party needed something from him more than he needed something from them. "The best thing you can do is deal from strength," Trump wrote in *The Art of the Deal*, "and leverage is the biggest strength you can have."

An early example of Trump's use of leverage was his acquisition of the Commodore Hotel in the late 1970s. The property, located near Grand Central Station, was in severe decline, and the

Penn Central Railroad, which owned it, was desperate to offload the asset as part of its bankruptcy proceedings. At the time, few developers saw potential in the aging hotel, but Trump recognized an opportunity. He knew that if he could secure the necessary financial backing and tax incentives, the hotel could be transformed into a high-end property that would attract tourists and business travelers alike.

Trump's leverage in this situation came from his ability to see value where others did not and his relationships with key players, including city officials. He positioned himself as the solution to New York's broader problem of urban decay, arguing that his redevelopment of the Commodore would spark a revitalization of the entire area. Trump used this narrative to negotiate a tax abatement deal with the city that dramatically reduced the financial burden of the project. By aligning his interests with the city's economic needs, he gained a powerful bargaining chip, making it difficult for officials to say no.

Timing, another critical element in Trump's negotiation playbook, was something he mastered early on. Trump believed that knowing when to strike was often more important than the details of the deal itself. Whether it was waiting for market conditions to turn in his favor or allowing the other party to feel the pressure of an impending deadline, Trump was a master at letting the clock work for him. In the case of the Commodore, Trump timed his negotiations with the city carefully, recognizing that officials were under pressure to show economic improvement and create jobs. This sense of urgency allowed him to secure favorable terms for the redevelopment project.

Another key tactic Trump used in negotiations was the willingness to walk away. While many dealmakers become emotionally attached to deals or afraid of losing out, Trump viewed walking away as a powerful negotiating tool. By demonstrating that he was

willing to let a deal fall through if the terms didn't meet his expectations, Trump often forced the other side to come back with
better offers. He understood that in many cases, the fear of losing a deal would push the other party to make concessions they
wouldn't have made otherwise. "You can't be afraid to walk away,"
Trump emphasized, "and you can't let anyone else see you sweat."

Trump's negotiations often extended beyond the boardroom
and into the public arena. He was highly skilled at using the media
to influence deals, turning press attention into a form of leverage.
By generating buzz around his projects and promoting himself as
a larger-than-life figure, Trump created public pressure that could
sway negotiations in his favor. In the case of the Commodore
Hotel, Trump publicly championed the redevelopment project,
framing it as essential to New York's revitalization. This media
narrative helped him gain public support and further increased the
pressure on city officials to approve his tax abatement request.

Trump also understood the importance of gathering informa-
tion and being thoroughly prepared for negotiations. He prided
himself on doing his homework, researching not just the details of
the deal but also the personalities and motivations of the people
he was negotiating with. This preparation allowed him to anticipate objections, counter arguments effectively, and sometimes
outmaneuver his opponents. Trump's ability to read people and
understand their interests was one of his greatest strengths in
negotiation. He recognized that deals weren't just about numbers—they were about relationships and the psychology of the individuals involved.

The negotiation of the Grand Hyatt deal, which transformed
the Commodore Hotel, became one of Trump's earliest major vic-
tories and set the tone for his future endeavors. His success in this
case was due not just to his ability to negotiate favorable terms but
also to his broader understanding of how to create value from a

distressed asset. By securing a 40-year tax abatement and financing the project with a mix of private and public funds, Trump was able to reduce his financial risk while ensuring long-term profitability for the hotel. The Grand Hyatt opened in 1980 and became a symbol of Trump's ability to turn ambitious visions into reality.

Throughout his career, Trump would continue to use the same negotiating tactics that had brought him early success. Whether he was dealing with contractors, lenders, or city officials, Trump always sought to find and maximize his leverage, time his negotiations to his advantage, and remain willing to walk away if necessary. His ability to navigate complex deals with a combination of preparation, boldness, and strategic thinking allowed him to achieve outcomes that others might have deemed impossible.

Negotiation, for Trump, wasn't just about closing a deal—it was about winning. And for Trump, winning meant not only securing the best possible terms but also reinforcing his reputation as a master dealmaker. His success in negotiation was a cornerstone of his business career and a key factor in building the empire that would bear his name.

Knowing When to Cut Losses and Walk Away

In the competitive landscape of business, one of the most critical skills a dealmaker can possess is the ability to recognize when a venture is no longer viable and to have the courage to walk away. For Donald Trump, this principle was not just theoretical; it was a fundamental part of his approach to business and a lesson he learned through experience. In *The Art of the Deal*, Trump emphasizes the importance of not becoming emotionally attached to any particular deal or project. His philosophy was clear: if the numbers didn't add up or the deal didn't align with his long-term goals, it was time to cut losses and move on.

This ability to recognize when to disengage became particularly evident during Trump's ventures into the world of Atlantic City casinos. In the late 1980s, Trump invested heavily in the burgeoning casino industry, believing it to be a golden opportunity to expand his empire. He opened Trump Plaza in 1984, followed by Trump's Castle and Trump Taj Mahal. Initially, these ventures were highly profitable, and Trump's star continued to rise as he became synonymous with luxury and entertainment in Atlantic City. However, the very nature of the casino business—its volatility and dependence on consumer spending—meant that this success was never guaranteed.

As competition in Atlantic City intensified and economic conditions shifted, Trump found himself facing increasing challenges. The financial burdens associated with running multiple casinos began to mount, and the industry experienced a downturn. By the early 1990s, Trump's casino empire was grappling with substantial debt and declining revenues. This was a critical juncture for Trump, and it required him to make tough decisions about the future of his investments.

Understanding when to cut losses became particularly relevant with the Taj Mahal, which Trump opened in 1990 with great fanfare. Marketed as the largest casino in the world, the Taj Mahal was a high-stakes gamble that required a massive investment. Trump anticipated that its grandeur would attract tourists and establish it as the centerpiece of his Atlantic City ventures. However, the project faced significant financial hurdles almost immediately, including overwhelming debt and operational costs that far exceeded projections.

Despite the initial excitement surrounding the Taj Mahal, Trump realized that the casino was struggling to meet its financial obligations. In *The Art of the Deal*, he reflects on the importance of recognizing when a project is not performing as expected, stating, "I'm not afraid to cut my losses. If something isn't working, it's better to walk away than to keep throwing good money after bad." This mindset proved crucial as Trump confronted the reality of the Taj Mahal's financial situation.

In 1991, Trump made the difficult decision to declare bankruptcy for the Taj Mahal and, ultimately, for his other casinos. This move was not taken lightly; it meant relinquishing control over projects he had poured his heart and soul into. However, Trump's willingness to walk away from underperforming ventures ultimately allowed him to preserve his personal wealth and reputation. By restructuring his debt and shedding unprofitable assets, he was able to stabilize his business interests and emerge from bankruptcy with a renewed focus on more promising opportunities.

This experience underscored a crucial lesson in Trump's approach to business: the importance of maintaining a pragmatic mindset. While many entrepreneurs may cling to their initial visions, fearing the stigma of failure, Trump recognized that the ability to adapt and pivot was vital for long-term success. He understood that walking away from a deal didn't equate to failure; instead, it demonstrated the ability to make calculated decisions based on the current realities of the market.

This principle was not limited to his ventures in Atlantic City; it permeated every aspect of Trump's business dealings. Whether negotiating real estate contracts, managing hotel renovations, or exploring new markets, he consistently evaluated the feasibility of each venture. In his discussions with investors and partners, he was candid about the potential risks and rewards of various projects, ensuring that all parties involved understood the stakes. By fostering an environment where honest assessments were valued, Trump cultivated a reputation for transparency—an essential quality in negotiations.

Another example of Trump's ability to cut losses can be seen in his handling of the Trump Shuttle, an airline service he launched in the late 1980s. Despite the initial enthusiasm surrounding the venture, Trump soon realized that the airline industry was fraught with challenges. Operational costs soared, competition was fierce, and profitability remained elusive. Understanding that the venture was not aligning with his overall business goals, Trump made the difficult decision to sell the airline. The move was both strategic and pragmatic, allowing him to recoup some of his initial investment while freeing up resources to focus on more lucrative projects.

Ultimately, Trump's experiences taught him that success in business often comes down to knowing when to hold on and when to let go. His willingness to cut losses and walk away from unproductive ventures became a defining characteristic of his approach to deal-making. It reinforced the idea that resilience and adaptability are essential traits for any entrepreneur navigating the unpredictable waters of business. For Trump, each decision to walk away was not a sign of defeat but rather a calculated step towards maintaining his overall vision and achieving long-term success.

In the world of business, where emotions can cloud judgment and the fear of failure looms large, Trump's commitment to recognizing when to disengage set him apart from many of his contemporaries. His ability to confront reality, reassess his investments, and make bold decisions allowed him to navigate some of the most tumultuous periods in his career while preserving his reputation and financial stability. In this way, Trump not only built an empire but also established a framework for sustainable success—one that emphasizes the importance of pragmatism and the courage to move forward, even when it means letting go.

Branding and the Power of Public Persona

One of the defining aspects of Donald Trump's business success is his acute understanding of branding and the power of public persona. Trump was not just a businessman; he was a brand in himself. From the outset of his career, he recognized that how he presented himself to the world would be just as critical as the quality of his real estate projects or the success of his business ventures. In *The Art of the Deal*, Trump explores the intricate dance between business and branding, illustrating how he leveraged his image to create an empire synonymous with luxury, success, and prestige.

At the heart of Trump's branding strategy was the idea that perception is reality. He understood that public opinion could significantly influence business outcomes, and he worked diligently to shape how he was perceived. Trump cultivated a persona that combined bravado, confidence, and an unmistakable flair for drama. His larger-than-life character became a powerful marketing tool, allowing him to differentiate himself in a crowded market. He positioned himself not merely as a businessman but as a cultural icon, someone who embodied the aspirational values of success and achievement.

The establishment of Trump Tower in 1983 marked a pivotal moment in this branding journey. This high-profile development wasn't just about constructing a luxury building; it was about creating a landmark that would signal Trump's arrival as a major player in New York real estate. With its gold-plated exterior and lavish atrium, Trump Tower became a symbol of opulence and wealth. The decision to make the building a mixed-use development—incorporating residential spaces, retail shops, and office suites—demonstrated Trump's understanding of market demands and his commitment to creating a multifaceted experience for visitors.

Moreover, Trump understood that the marketing of Trump Tower was as vital as the physical structure itself. He leveraged media coverage to amplify the building's visibility, staging grand openings and celebrity events that attracted attention from both the press and potential buyers. Trump became a fixture in the media, often appearing in interviews and on talk shows to discuss his ventures and promote his brand. By positioning himself as the face of Trump Tower, he ensured that his name was intrinsically linked to the success of the project.

Trump's branding strategy extended beyond individual properties; it encompassed the creation of a personal brand that would resonate with audiences far and wide. He carefully crafted his image to embody the ideals of success and power, appealing to a demographic that aspired to wealth and luxury. This was especially significant in the 1980s, a decade marked by economic prosperity and a growing fascination with the lifestyles of the rich and famous. Trump capitalized on this cultural moment, portraying himself as a self-made mogul who achieved success against all odds.

His ability to create a compelling narrative around his persona was instrumental in his brand-building efforts. Trump's story was not merely about financial success; it was about the American dream—a narrative that resonated with many aspiring entrepreneurs and individuals seeking inspiration. He portrayed himself as a quintessential example of what one could achieve through hard work, determination, and a little bit of audacity. This narrative was not just a marketing tool; it was a reflection of his belief in his own capabilities and his commitment to realizing his ambitions.

As Trump expanded his brand, he recognized the importance of diversifying his ventures to enhance his public persona further. In addition to real estate, he ventured into various industries, including entertainment, hospitality, and consumer products. The

launch of the Trump University, though later mired in controversy, was an effort to tap into the education market while reinforcing his image as an authority on success and wealth creation.
Similarly, his involvement in the reality television show *The Apprentice* transformed Trump from a businessman into a household
name. The show provided him with a platform to showcase his
business acumen while entertaining audiences, solidifying his status as a cultural icon.

Through *The Apprentice*, Trump crafted a carefully controlled
image, balancing the roles of mentor and tough taskmaster. The
show's success reinforced his brand, as viewers came to associate
his name with both entertainment and business prowess. This
crossover appeal was critical in maintaining his relevance in an
ever-evolving media landscape. The series not only garnered high
ratings but also created an avenue for Trump to extend his brand
into new territories, including merchandise and public speaking
engagements.

However, branding is not without its pitfalls, and Trump's
journey was no exception. The high-profile nature of his businesses made him a frequent target for criticism and scrutiny. As
he expanded his brand, he faced challenges related to public perception, particularly concerning the quality and consistency of his
ventures. While the Trump name became synonymous with luxury, there were instances where projects failed to meet expectations, leading to legal disputes and reputational damage. Yet,
Trump's resilience allowed him to weather these storms; he con-
tinuously rebranded and adapted to maintain his public persona.

In *The Art of the Deal*, Trump asserts, "If you're going to be
thinking anyway, you might as well think big." This sentiment underscored his approach to branding, where every deal and every
venture was an opportunity to reinforce his image. His relentless
focus on branding and public persona enabled him to navigate the

complexities of business while building a legacy that transcended the real estate market.

Ultimately, Trump's ability to intertwine his personal brand with his business ventures played a crucial role in his success. By creating an image that resonated with the public and promoting his projects through a lens of aspiration and luxury, he transformed himself into a cultural phenomenon. The lessons he learned about the power of branding, media, and public perception would continue to influence his business strategies long after his early ventures. In this way, Trump not only built an empire of real estate and entertainment but also crafted a lasting brand that would leave an indelible mark on American culture.

Leveraging Media and Publicity

In an age defined by the 24-hour news cycle and the explosion of social media, the ability to leverage media and publicity can make or break a business. Donald Trump understood this concept intuitively, often asserting that publicity—whether good or bad—was a vital component of his branding strategy. Throughout his career, Trump has demonstrated an uncanny ability to manipulate media coverage to his advantage, turning headlines into opportunities that would bolster his public persona and, in turn, his business ventures.

From his early days in real estate, Trump recognized the power of the press. He understood that being in the news could elevate his profile and keep his name at the forefront of public consciousness. This realization became particularly evident with the launch of Trump Tower. The building's grand opening in 1983 was not merely a celebration of a new luxury property; it was an event meticulously orchestrated to attract media attention. Trump invited celebrities, politicians, and influential figures, creating a star-studded atmosphere that ensured the event was covered extensively. The media frenzy surrounding the opening allowed Trump to position Trump Tower not just as a building but as a cultural milestone.

Moreover, Trump's willingness to engage with the media was a calculated decision rooted in a deep understanding of public relations. He often made himself available for interviews, utilizing platforms like talk shows and news programs to promote his projects. His charismatic personality and brash style resonated with audiences, making him a sought-after guest. In these appearances, Trump effectively portrayed himself as a self-made man who achieved success through hard work and an unrelenting pursuit of excellence. By controlling the narrative surrounding his ventures, he ensured that his brand was consistently associated with success and ambition.

Another hallmark of Trump's media strategy was his adeptness at generating controversy. While many business leaders shy away from conflict, Trump embraced it, often positioning himself at the center of public debates. This approach not only kept him in the headlines but also reinforced his brand as someone who was unafraid to challenge the status quo. For instance, during the early 1990s, when his Atlantic City casinos faced financial difficulties, Trump openly discussed his challenges and framed them as part of the broader narrative of a determined entrepreneur fighting against adversity. By doing so, he transformed potential setbacks into compelling stories of resilience, capturing public interest and sympathy.

Trump also understood that sensationalism sells. He often employed provocative language and bold statements to capture media attention. His infamous catchphrases—"You're fired!" from *The Apprentice* and "Make America Great Again" during his political campaign—became rallying cries that encapsulated his brand.

These memorable slogans not only made headlines but also fostered a sense of loyalty among supporters, creating a dedicated audience that would advocate for his projects and ventures. Trump recognized that soundbites and slogans could transcend individual deals, embedding his brand into the cultural zeitgeist.

As Trump's brand expanded, so did his media presence. He began to leverage not only traditional media outlets but also the burgeoning world of social media. With the rise of platforms like Twitter and Facebook, Trump found new avenues to communicate directly with the public. He embraced these platforms, using them to share his thoughts, promote his businesses, and, at times, stir controversy. By bypassing traditional media gatekeepers, Trump could control his narrative and engage directly with his audience, fostering a sense of intimacy and immediacy that resonated with many.

However, Trump's media strategy was not without risks. His penchant for controversy and unabashed self-promotion sometimes drew criticism and backlash. In an era of increasing scrutiny, Trump faced challenges related to the ethical implications of his media engagement. Critics argued that his tactics often blurred the line between reality and spectacle, raising questions about the authenticity of his persona. Yet, for Trump, the potential risks were outweighed by the rewards of heightened visibility and brand recognition.

Ultimately, Trump's ability to leverage media and publicity became one of the cornerstones of his business strategy. He transformed the way entrepreneurs approached public relations, demonstrating that a well-crafted narrative, combined with strategic media engagement, could elevate a brand to new heights. By turning himself into a media-savvy mogul, Trump not only built an empire of properties and businesses but also created a legacy as a cultural phenomenon.

In *The Art of the Deal*, Trump encapsulates this philosophy succinctly: "It's better to be talked about than not talked about." This mantra guided his interactions with the media, leading him to embrace controversy and cultivate an image that would captivate public interest. Through careful planning and execution, Trump transformed his name into a brand that resonated with millions, proving that the right media strategy could propel a business to unprecedented success.

The lessons learned from Trump's media maneuvers are invaluable for any aspiring entrepreneur. In an era where attention is a scarce resource, the ability to craft a compelling narrative, engage with the public, and leverage media coverage is essential for success. Trump's journey illustrates that in the world of business, perception often matters just as much as reality. By harnessing the power of media and cultivating a public persona that resonates with audiences, entrepreneurs can build brands that withstand the test of time. In this way, Trump not only exemplified the power of media in business but also redefined the relationship between branding, publicity, and success.

| 6 |

Chapter 6: Expanding Globally: Trump International

The Vision for Global Expansion

From the very beginning of his career, Donald Trump harbored an ambitious vision that extended far beyond the confines of the United States. He understood that in order to build a truly formidable empire, he would need to leverage the immense potential offered by international markets. The late 20th century, characterized by rapid globalization and the emergence of new economic powerhouses, presented an unprecedented opportunity for those willing to think big. Trump was one of those individuals, and his desire for global expansion would soon become a hallmark of his business strategy.

Trump's fascination with luxury and success fueled his ambitions. He envisioned his brand not merely as a collection of properties but as a lifestyle that epitomized the aspirational ideals of wealth and prestige. As the world became more interconnected, Trump recognized that the allure of luxury living was not confined to American shores. Emerging economies in Asia, the Middle East, and parts of Europe were beginning to witness a surge in affluence, creating a ripe environment for luxury real estate development. It was in this context that Trump began to strategize how to position his brand on a global scale.

The notion of expanding the Trump brand internationally was not just about geographical reach; it was also about brand identity. Trump wanted his name to be synonymous with high-end living, and he understood that to achieve this, he needed to tap into the growing demand for luxury accommodations in key cities around the world. As the global economy flourished, so did the aspirations of the wealthy class, who sought out luxurious experiences in travel and leisure. For Trump, this represented a perfect alignment of opportunity and ambition.

With this vision in mind, Trump began to explore the possibility of establishing Trump International as a global brand. His approach was multi-faceted. First, he sought partnerships with established developers and investors in international markets. He understood that while his name carried weight, local expertise was invaluable in navigating unfamiliar landscapes. By forging these alliances, Trump could minimize risk while maximizing the potential for success. His initial foray into international markets would rely heavily on collaboration and shared resources, allowing him to leverage the strengths of both his brand and local players.

Furthermore, Trump was acutely aware of the changing dynamics of global wealth. The rise of the affluent middle class in countries like China and India presented an unprecedented opportunity for luxury brands. He recognized that the demand for high-end real estate and accommodations was increasing in regions that had previously been overlooked by American developers. By positioning himself early in these burgeoning markets, Trump aimed to establish the Trump brand as the go-to choice for luxury living in emerging economies.

As part of his strategic planning, Trump began to identify key markets for expansion. Major cities such as London, Dubai, and Shanghai became focal points in his vision for a global empire. These cities not only boasted a wealth of potential clients but also served as international hubs for commerce and tourism. By targeting these markets, Trump sought to create a network of Trump-branded properties that would elevate his global profile and further solidify his brand's association with luxury.

In addition to market selection, Trump also focused on the architectural vision of his international projects. He understood that the physical manifestation of the Trump brand needed to reflect the opulence and grandeur that his name conveyed. Each new property was designed not just as a building but as a statement—a beacon of luxury that would attract attention and clientele alike. Trump envisioned properties that would stand as iconic landmarks in their respective cities, combining cutting-edge design with the trademark flair associated with his brand.

Ultimately, Trump's vision for global expansion was a reflection of his belief in the power of branding, strategic partnerships, and market foresight. He recognized that success in the global arena required not only a bold vision but also a willingness to adapt and learn from local cultures. As he began to implement this vision, the groundwork was laid for the Trump International brand to take flight, setting the stage for a new chapter in his entrepreneurial journey.

This point underscores that Trump's journey into global expansion was driven by a combination of ambition, strategic insight, and a keen awareness of the shifting tides of wealth and consumer behavior. By positioning himself to capitalize on these trends, he not only sought to grow his empire but also aimed to redefine what it meant to be a global brand in the luxury market. In doing so, Trump was not just expanding his business; he was carving out a legacy that would resonate across borders and cultures, marking the Trump brand as a prominent player on the world stage.

Establishing Trump International Hotels and Towers

The launch of Trump International Hotels and Towers represented a pivotal moment in Donald Trump's quest for global dominance in the luxury hospitality sector. As he sought to elevate his brand beyond the confines of the United States, Trump recognized that creating a line of luxury hotels and residences would not only diversify his business portfolio but also solidify his reputation as a global real estate mogul. This strategic move aimed to blend opulence with functionality, catering to affluent travelers and discerning residents around the world.

The first significant project that marked the establishment of the Trump International brand was the Trump International Hotel and Tower in Toronto, Canada. Opened in 2012, this luxurious skyscraper was designed to embody the essence of high-end living and served as a critical proof of concept for Trump's international ambitions. Located in the heart of downtown Toronto, the property featured upscale condominiums, a five-star hotel, fine dining, and a lavish spa—all designed to offer guests and residents an unparalleled experience. Trump's vision was to create a space that not only dazzled with its architecture but also provided top-notch service, positioning the hotel as a destination in itself.

The architectural design of the Toronto tower was a critical component of Trump's strategy. Collaborating with renowned architects and designers, Trump aimed to ensure that each property under the Trump International brand would stand out in the competitive luxury market. The Toronto tower was adorned with a sleek, modern façade that captured the city's skyline, establishing it as a new symbol of luxury in Canada. This commitment to excellence in design was crucial, as Trump understood that luxury travelers often sought unique experiences that went beyond mere accommodation. By incorporating distinctive design elements and high-end amenities, Trump aimed to create a lasting impression that would resonate with international guests.

Following the success of the Toronto project, Trump set his sights on other major cities around the globe. The Trump International Hotel and Tower in Dubai became a flagship property that showcased his brand's global reach. Opened in 2010, this luxury hotel was situated in the heart of one of the world's fastest-growing cities, and it featured the lavish amenities and world-class service that were hallmarks of the Trump brand. Trump's strategic choice to enter the Dubai market highlighted his ability to recognize and capitalize on emerging luxury destinations, further solidifying his reputation as a savvy entrepreneur.

However, establishing a global hotel brand was not without its challenges. As Trump ventured into international markets, he encountered diverse regulatory environments, varying consumer preferences, and fierce competition. In response, Trump relied on a combination of thorough market research and local partnerships to navigate these complexities. By collaborating with established local developers and investors, he could mitigate risks associated with entering new markets while gaining valuable insights into consumer behavior.

One notable partnership was with the Dubai-based Nakheel Properties for the development of the Trump International Hotel and Tower in Dubai. This alliance allowed Trump to leverage Nakheel's local expertise and extensive network, facilitating a smoother entry into the Middle Eastern market. By forming strategic alliances, Trump was able to maintain his brand's high standards while adapting to local market demands, effectively blending global luxury with regional influences.

As Trump International Hotels and Towers expanded into new markets, the brand began to establish itself as a premier choice for luxury accommodations. Each property was designed to cater to affluent clientele, offering not just rooms but also lifestyle experiences. High-end dining options, lavish spas, and exclusive events became staples of the Trump International brand, reinforcing its position as a symbol of luxury living.

In addition to physical properties, Trump's brand was marketed through strategic advertising campaigns that emphasized the aspirational lifestyle associated with Trump International. High-profile events, celebrity endorsements, and carefully curated marketing materials helped to create an image of exclusivity and prestige. The Trump brand began to resonate not only with wealthy travelers but also with those aspiring to experience the luxury lifestyle associated with Trump's name.

Throughout this expansion, Trump remained deeply involved in the branding and marketing of his properties. He understood that maintaining the integrity of the Trump name was paramount, and he was vigilant in ensuring that each new venture adhered to the high standards he had established. This hands-on approach not only elevated the brand but also reinforced his image as a dedicated and passionate entrepreneur.

As Trump International Hotels and Towers continued to flourish, the impact of these ventures on Trump's overall brand became increasingly apparent. Each successful property added to the allure of the Trump name, positioning it as a leader in luxury real estate and hospitality. By establishing a robust portfolio of international hotels, Trump was not only creating lucrative business opportunities but also laying the groundwork for a legacy that would resonate long after he stepped away from day-to-day operations.

In summary, the establishment of Trump International Hotels and Towers marked a significant milestone in Donald Trump's global expansion strategy. By launching luxurious properties in key international markets, he was able to leverage his brand recognition while creating a standard of excellence in hospitality. Through strategic partnerships, meticulous attention to design, and a focus on providing unique experiences, Trump laid the foundation for a global brand that would become synonymous with luxury and prestige. This venture not only diversified his business interests but also cemented his status as a formidable player on the world stage, showcasing the power of branding in the pursuit of international success.

The Role of Licensing Agreements

As Donald Trump sought to expand his international footprint, he recognized that direct investment in every potential market was neither feasible nor necessary. Instead, he turned to licensing agreements as a strategic tool to extend the Trump brand without the substantial financial risk associated with full ownership of every property. This approach allowed him to capitalize on the appeal of his name and the allure of his brand while leveraging the expertise of local developers and investors who understood their markets intimately.

Licensing agreements became a cornerstone of Trump's global expansion strategy. By allowing developers to use the Trump name and branding in exchange for a fee or a share of the profits, Trump was able to enter new markets with significantly reduced risk. This arrangement was particularly advantageous in regions where local knowledge was paramount. For instance, in countries like Indonesia and the Philippines, Trump licensed his brand to established real estate firms that could navigate the complexities of local regulations and cultural preferences. This model not only facilitated rapid expansion but also allowed Trump to maintain a level of quality and brand integrity without overextending his financial resources.

One of the most notable licensing agreements was struck in 2013 when Trump partnered with a consortium of developers to create Trump Tower Manila, a luxurious residential condominium in the Philippines. This development was aimed at the rapidly growing affluent class in Southeast Asia, a market that was burgeoning with opportunities. By leveraging the Trump brand, the developers were able to attract buyers seeking high-end living in a city known for its vibrant culture and economic growth. Trump's involvement added a layer of prestige to the project, making it an attractive option for affluent buyers who sought not only a residence but also a status symbol.

The licensing strategy extended beyond just residential properties; it also encompassed hotel developments and commercial real estate. In 2015, Trump signed a licensing agreement with a developer in Dubai for a luxury hotel and residential project that would bear the Trump name. This agreement allowed the developer to utilize Trump's brand, design aesthetic, and operational standards while reducing Trump's direct financial involvement. The result was a highly lucrative project that enhanced the Trump brand's reputation in the Middle East while minimizing risk.

However, while licensing agreements provided significant opportunities, they also came with challenges. The most critical of these was the necessity to maintain brand integrity. Trump was keenly aware that his name represented a promise of quality and luxury, and any deviation from that standard could tarnish his reputation. To mitigate this risk, Trump implemented strict guidelines for licensed properties. These guidelines encompassed everything from architectural design to service standards, ensuring that every property bearing the Trump name met his rigorous expectations.

In addition to maintaining quality, Trump had to navigate the complexities of relationships with local partners. The success of a licensed property depended heavily on the capabilities and reliability of the local developers. Trump carefully selected partners with a proven track record in their respective markets. This emphasis on collaboration was essential, as it allowed him to forge strong alliances that would support the long-term success of the Trump brand internationally.

Marketing also played a crucial role in the success of licensed properties. Each new development under the Trump name was accompanied by high-profile marketing campaigns that highlighted the unique features of the project while emphasizing the luxury and prestige associated with the Trump brand. By leveraging media attention and celebrity endorsements, Trump was able to create buzz around new properties, drawing in potential buyers and investors eager to associate with the glamorous lifestyle the brand represented.

The financial implications of licensing agreements were significant. They allowed Trump to generate income from a variety of global sources without the need for substantial capital investment. As each licensed property became operational, it contributed to a growing revenue stream that enhanced Trump's overall financial position. Moreover, successful projects added to the brand's prestige, creating a cycle of demand that further fueled expansion.

While licensing agreements proved to be a fruitful strategy for international growth, they were not without their pitfalls. Some licensed ventures faced challenges that led to underperformance or reputational risk. In such cases, Trump had to make difficult decisions about whether to continue supporting a struggling project or to distance himself from it entirely. This balance between expansion and brand preservation was delicate, but Trump's experience in the business world equipped him to navigate these complexities.

Overall, licensing agreements emerged as a key component of Donald Trump's strategy for global expansion. By leveraging the expertise of local partners and minimizing financial risks, he was able to expand the Trump brand into diverse markets while maintaining a commitment to quality and luxury. This approach allowed him to navigate the complexities of international business effectively, establishing a robust global presence that would resonate with affluent consumers around the world. Through this model, Trump not only expanded his business empire but also solidified his identity as a global brand, demonstrating the power of licensing as a strategy for entrepreneurial success.

Navigating Challenges in Global Markets

While Donald Trump's vision for global expansion was ambitious, the journey was not without its challenges. Entering international markets introduced complexities that demanded a strategic approach and a nuanced understanding of various cultural, economic, and regulatory landscapes. As Trump International sought to establish a foothold in diverse regions, it encountered obstacles ranging from economic downturns and geopolitical tensions to differing consumer preferences and local market dynamics.

One of the most significant challenges Trump faced was the variability of economic conditions across different countries. The global financial crisis of 2008 served as a sobering reminder of the fragility of international markets. As consumer confidence plummeted, luxury real estate sales took a hit, and many developers found themselves in precarious positions. For Trump, this period posed a dual challenge: maintaining the integrity of his brand while also managing the expectations of investors and stakeholders. Despite the economic downturn, Trump remained committed to his international expansion plans, viewing the crisis as an opportunity to position his brand for long-term success.

During this tumultuous period, Trump focused on fortifying relationships with his partners and local developers. He understood that collaboration would be vital to navigating the financial landscape. By working closely with local stakeholders, he sought to adapt his strategies to meet the changing demands of the market. This required a level of flexibility that was sometimes at odds with his established brand identity, but Trump was willing to make concessions in order to sustain growth. For example, during the downturn, he agreed to revise some of the terms in licensing agreements to support struggling partners, thereby fostering goodwill and loyalty.

In addition to economic fluctuations, Trump had to contend with the complexities of navigating different regulatory environments. Each country presented unique legal frameworks, zoning laws, and business practices that required thorough understanding and adaptation. For instance, when expanding into the European market, Trump faced stringent regulations regarding construction and environmental standards that differed significantly from those in the United States. Understanding these differences was crucial for avoiding legal pitfalls that could jeopardize projects.

To address these challenges, Trump engaged local legal and regulatory experts to ensure compliance with all requirements. This approach not only mitigated risk but also facilitated smoother project approvals. By investing in local expertise, Trump demonstrated his commitment to operating responsibly and sustainably within each market. This strategy ultimately helped to build credibility and trust with local authorities and communities, essential elements for any successful international venture.

Cultural differences also posed challenges that Trump had to navigate thoughtfully. The preferences and expectations of luxury consumers can vary widely from one region to another. What appeals to affluent buyers in New York may not resonate with potential customers in Dubai or Shanghai. Trump recognized the importance of tailoring marketing strategies and product offerings to align with local tastes. In the Middle East, for example, the design of Trump-branded properties incorporated elements of local architecture and aesthetics, ensuring that they not only appealed to international buyers but also resonated with local culture.

Additionally, Trump often found himself in the spotlight of global media, and public perception could greatly influence the success of his ventures. His polarizing persona, shaped by his outspoken nature and high-profile political aspirations, sometimes created skepticism among potential investors and customers overseas. Understanding the importance of reputation management, Trump took steps to reinforce the brand's commitment to quality and luxury, countering any negative perceptions through strategic public relations campaigns. High-profile openings and media events served as opportunities to showcase the Trump brand in a positive light, emphasizing its exclusivity and appeal.

Geopolitical tensions also impacted Trump's international ventures. Trade disputes, political instability, and changes in government policies could create uncertainty in various markets. For example, as tensions between the United States and China escalated in the late 2010s, Trump faced scrutiny regarding his business interests in the region. Navigating this landscape required a deft approach, balancing his business pursuits with the realities of international relations.

Despite these challenges, Trump's determination to expand globally remained unwavering. He leveraged his resilience and adaptability to navigate the complexities of international markets, continually refining his strategies based on market feedback and evolving trends. By maintaining a proactive approach and staying attuned to global developments, Trump positioned himself to respond to challenges with agility, turning potential setbacks into opportunities for growth.

Ultimately, the journey of establishing Trump International across the globe underscored the importance of resilience, adaptability, and strategic collaboration. Through his experiences, Trump demonstrated that success in international markets requires not only a bold vision but also the ability to navigate the intricacies of diverse environments. The challenges he faced became valuable lessons that would shape his approach to business and international relations, reinforcing his reputation as a savvy entrepreneur who could thrive in an ever-changing global landscape.

As he continued to expand the Trump brand, Trump's commitment to quality, collaboration, and cultural understanding became key tenets of his strategy. These principles not only helped him navigate the complexities of global markets but also solidified his legacy as a formidable force in the world of luxury real estate and hospitality. Each challenge he encountered served to reinforce his resolve and commitment to building an empire that would stand the test of time.

The Legacy of Trump International

As Donald Trump's international ventures unfolded, the impact of Trump International on the global luxury market became increasingly evident. The brand evolved into a symbol of opulence and aspiration, appealing to affluent consumers around the world.

By strategically leveraging licensing agreements, cultivating strong partnerships, and navigating the complexities of international markets, Trump successfully positioned his brand as a leader in luxury hospitality and real estate. However, the true measure of success lies not only in the financial gains but also in the legacy established through these global endeavors.

One of the most notable aspects of Trump International's legacy is its contribution to the luxury real estate landscape. The brand set new standards for what consumers could expect from high-end hotels and residences. Each Trump property was meticulously designed to embody luxury, featuring state-of-the-art amenities, breathtaking views, and exceptional service. The brand became synonymous with exclusivity, drawing in celebrities, dignitaries, and affluent travelers who sought more than just a place to stay; they sought an experience that reflected their status and lifestyle.

Trump's influence on the luxury market extended beyond the physical properties themselves. His ability to market the Trump brand as a lifestyle became a powerful tool in shaping consumer perceptions. High-profile marketing campaigns showcased not just the properties but also the aspirational lifestyle associated with them. By intertwining his name with luxury experiences, Trump cultivated a brand identity that resonated deeply with wealthy consumers, creating a desire for association with the Trump name. This branding strategy became a blueprint for future luxury ventures, influencing how brands marketed themselves in the competitive global marketplace.

The legacy of Trump International also includes its role in fostering economic growth and development in various regions. The construction and operation of luxury properties often had a ripple effect on local economies, creating jobs and generating revenue for surrounding businesses. In many cases, Trump's projects helped to revitalize struggling neighborhoods, attracting tourists and residents alike. The Trump brand became a catalyst for urban development, showcasing how luxury projects could elevate local economies while enhancing the overall landscape.

Furthermore, Trump International's global expansion highlighted the interconnectedness of the modern economy. As Trump navigated different markets, he demonstrated the importance of understanding local cultures and adapting to regional preferences. His approach to international business underscored the necessity of collaboration and partnership in an increasingly globalized world. By recognizing and respecting local customs, Trump was able to build bridges that facilitated successful ventures and fostered goodwill among communities.

However, the legacy of Trump International was not without its controversies. The brand often found itself at the center of heated debates regarding business ethics, environmental impact, and social responsibility. Critics pointed to the potential for luxury developments to exacerbate social inequalities and contribute to environmental degradation. In response, Trump began to address these concerns by emphasizing sustainable practices in some of his projects and promoting community engagement. This evolution in approach showcased a growing awareness of the responsibilities that come with operating a global brand.

As Trump International continued to expand, the brand also became a focal point for discussions about the role of celebrity in business. Trump's larger-than-life persona, coupled with his reality television fame, added a unique dimension to his brand's identity. This blending of entertainment and entrepreneurship captivated audiences, allowing Trump to leverage his media presence to bolster his business ventures. The intersection of celebrity culture and business became a key aspect of the Trump legacy, influencing how entrepreneurs approached branding and marketing in the modern era.

In reflecting on the legacy of Trump International, it is essential to acknowledge the impact of global events on the brand's evolution. As geopolitical landscapes shifted and global markets fluctuated, Trump's adaptability became a defining characteristic of his approach. His ability to pivot and seize opportunities in the face of adversity showcased the resilience necessary for sustained success in a competitive environment.

Ultimately, the legacy of Trump International extends beyond mere financial success. It encompasses a broader narrative of ambition, innovation, and the pursuit of excellence in the luxury market. Trump's ventures not only transformed his own brand but also influenced the global landscape of luxury real estate and hospitality. The properties bearing the Trump name became emblematic of a lifestyle that many aspired to achieve, reflecting the intersection of wealth, status, and experience.

In conclusion, the story of Trump International is one of ambition and determination, marked by both triumphs and challenges. Through strategic partnerships, innovative branding, and an unwavering commitment to quality, Donald Trump established a legacy that would leave an indelible mark on the luxury market. The brand's influence continues to resonate, serving as a testament to the power of entrepreneurship and the potential for creating a global legacy through vision and perseverance. As Trump International forges ahead, its impact on the world of luxury real estate and hospitality will be felt for generations to come, solidifying Donald Trump's position as a prominent figure in the landscape of global business.

| 7 |

Chapter 7: Branding Genius: Trump as a Global Bran

The Birth of the Trump Brand

The Trump name has become synonymous with luxury, power, and success, but the journey to establishing Donald Trump as a global brand began long before the world knew him as a media personality or politician. It all started with a keen understanding of the value of perception, something Donald Trump recognized early in his career as a young real estate developer in New York City. While Trump initially built his empire on bricks, mortar, and steel, he quickly realized that the most valuable asset in his portfolio wasn't physical—it was his name.

The Trump brand was born out of the same entrepreneurial spirit that guided his father, Fred Trump, who built a successful real estate business focused on middle-income housing in the outer boroughs of New York. However, from the start, Donald had his sights set on something far grander. He wasn't content to follow in his father's footsteps; he wanted to create something bigger, more iconic, and more glamorous. This desire to rise above the conventional real estate world and make a lasting mark on

Manhattan's skyline was the genesis of what would become one of the most recognizable personal brands in history.

In the mid-1970s, Donald Trump embarked on his first major project in Manhattan: the transformation of the Commodore Hotel into the Grand Hyatt. This project marked a pivotal moment in his career. He wasn't just redeveloping a property; he was crafting a persona. He insisted that his name be prominently featured in the media coverage surrounding the project, ensuring that every mention of the Grand Hyatt also included the name "Trump." For Donald, it wasn't enough to be a successful developer—he wanted the public to associate his name with success itself.

Trump understood that perception is reality in the business world. By positioning himself as a larger-than-life figure, he cultivated an aura of success, ambition, and luxury that would become the foundation of his brand. The Trump name became synonymous with bold deals and high-stakes ventures. Even when his projects faced difficulties, Trump skillfully used his charm and media savvy to keep the narrative focused on his triumphs rather than setbacks.

One of the earliest indications of Trump's branding genius came with the construction of Trump Tower, which opened in 1983. The gleaming 68-story skyscraper on Fifth Avenue was not just a real estate project—it was a statement. The building's shimmering bronze glass façade, luxurious interiors, and opulent marble atrium were all carefully designed to project an image of unparalleled luxury. But more important than the building itself was the name emblazoned across it: "Trump." This marked a shift in Trump's business strategy. He was no longer just building buildings—he was building his name into an icon of luxury real estate.

From this point on, Donald Trump made sure his name was at the forefront of every venture. The Trump brand was more than a signature—it was a symbol of quality and prestige. As he expanded his real estate holdings throughout New York and beyond, Trump understood that his personal name carried weight, attracting not just investors and buyers, but also media attention. Every time he appeared in the press or on television, he was reinforcing the image of Donald Trump as a larger-than-life figure, one whose name was synonymous with success.

However, Trump's branding prowess wasn't limited to physical properties. He understood the potential for his name to transcend real estate and enter the broader consciousness as a symbol of achievement and ambition. By attaching his name to high-profile properties in New York, Trump was building not just a business, but an identity that could be leveraged in countless ways. He cultivated an image of boldness, luxury, and grandiosity that made people take notice, even those who had no direct connection to the real estate market.

Trump's early branding efforts weren't without risk. By attaching his name so prominently to his projects, he ensured that his successes and failures were both equally public. If a project faltered, it wasn't just a building that was affected—it was the Trump name. Yet this risk only made his brand more powerful. Trump's willingness to take bold chances and place his reputation on the line became part of the allure. His brand wasn't just about success; it was about audacity, the willingness to pursue grand visions no matter the obstacles.

By the early 1980s, the Trump brand was firmly established in the world of New York real estate. But this was just the beginning. Donald Trump had laid the groundwork for a brand that would eventually expand far beyond Manhattan, reaching across industries and into global markets. He had positioned his name as a marker of ambition and luxury, a symbol that would carry him into the worlds of media, entertainment, and international business. The birth of the Trump brand was not just the beginning of a business empire—it was the start of a global phenomenon.

From Real Estate to Lifestyle

As Donald Trump's real estate empire grew, so did his ambitions for the Trump name. He realized early on that his brand could transcend the physical properties he was developing. Trump wasn't just building skyscrapers; he was building an image—one that embodied wealth, luxury, and success. This realization marked a significant turning point in his career. The Trump brand would soon evolve from being a name on buildings to representing an entire lifestyle.

In the late 1980s, Trump began to explore how his name could extend beyond the realm of real estate. He had already solidified his reputation in New York City with projects like Trump Tower and the Grand Hyatt, but now, he wanted to create a lifestyle brand that could touch different aspects of people's lives. Trump understood that if he could associate his name with luxury living, the brand could enter industries beyond real estate, reaching into hospitality, entertainment, and consumer products.

One of Trump's first major ventures outside real estate was the casino business. With the opening of Trump Plaza and Trump Taj Mahal in Atlantic City, he demonstrated his ability to apply the Trump brand to an entirely new sector. The casinos weren't just places to gamble—they were entertainment hubs, designed to immerse visitors in an experience of extravagance and opulence. Everything, from the marble-clad interiors to the high-end restaurants, was carefully curated to reflect the luxurious lifestyle that Trump had built his brand around. These casinos became extensions of the Trump image, blending high stakes with high glamour, and helping to cement Trump's reputation as a purveyor of luxury entertainment.

Trump's foray into the hospitality industry marked another critical expansion of his brand. As he developed high-end hotels and resorts, he saw an opportunity to infuse the Trump name into the luxury travel experience. Trump hotels weren't just accommodations—they were destinations in their own right, offering a level of service and sophistication that catered to the world's elite. Properties like Trump International Hotel and Tower in New York and the Trump International Hotel Las Vegas became synonymous with luxury, attracting wealthy travelers who sought not just comfort but prestige.

What made Trump's branding approach unique was his emphasis on creating a lifestyle. He wasn't just selling hotel rooms or casino experiences; he was selling the idea of living like Donald Trump. The Trump name became a symbol of aspiration for those who wanted to live lavishly and succeed on a grand scale. Whether staying at a Trump hotel, visiting a Trump casino, or eventually purchasing Trump-branded products, consumers were buying into a vision of success that Trump had carefully crafted.

By the early 1990s, Trump had expanded his reach into the world of consumer products. He licensed the Trump name to a variety of goods, including high-end furniture, cologne, clothing, and even bottled water. These ventures capitalized on Trump's growing celebrity status and reinforced the idea that the Trump lifestyle could be accessible to anyone willing to pay the price. Owning a piece of the Trump brand, whether it was a bottle of cologne or a furniture set, allowed consumers to feel like they were part of an exclusive club—one defined by luxury and success.

The most important aspect of this expansion was Trump's ability to maintain consistency across his brand. Whether it was real estate, hotels, or products, every venture that bore the Trump name had to adhere to the same principles of luxury, exclusivity, and high quality. Trump personally oversaw many of these developments, ensuring that his brand's reputation remained intact. He understood that in order for the Trump brand to thrive, it needed to be more than just a collection of successful businesses—it had to represent a cohesive lifestyle.

Part of Trump's success in this area was his ability to market himself alongside his products. Trump wasn't just a businessman; he was the embodiment of the brand. His larger-than-life persona, showcased in interviews, television appearances, and books like *The Art of the Deal*, made him not only a real estate mogul but also a celebrity. Trump's fame allowed him to promote his ventures in ways that other businesspeople couldn't. His personal life, business triumphs, and bold personality were all part of the brand narrative. Consumers didn't just want a Trump product—they wanted a piece of Trump's world, a world where success seemed limitless and luxury was the norm.

By successfully attaching his name to a wide array of industries, Trump transformed the Trump brand into a full-fledged lifestyle empire. It wasn't just about buildings or casinos anymore. The Trump brand had grown into a global symbol of success, representing a certain kind of aspirational living. From real estate to fashion, from hotels to consumer goods, the Trump name had become synonymous with luxury and affluence, appealing to people who aspired to live like Trump—or at least, to project the image of such a life.

Ultimately, the expansion of the Trump brand beyond real estate marked the beginning of Donald Trump's evolution into a global icon. He had tapped into the psychology of aspiration, offering consumers more than just products and services—he was offering them an image, a dream, a lifestyle. The ability to create a brand that was more than the sum of its parts was a testament to Trump's branding genius. His ventures in lifestyle branding not only diversified his business interests but also laid the foundation for what would become one of the most recognizable brands in the world.

The Role of Media in Building the Trump Brand

The media has always been a powerful tool in shaping public perception, and no one understood this better than Donald Trump. From the early days of his career, Trump demonstrated a unique ability to leverage the media to promote his ventures, his brand, and ultimately, himself. By cultivating a constant presence in newspapers, magazines, and television, he transformed from a successful real estate developer into a global icon. His savvy use of media played a pivotal role in building the Trump brand, elevating his name beyond the realm of business and into the broader public consciousness.

One of Trump's earliest and most significant media triumphs was his relationship with New York City's press. In the 1970s and 1980s, Trump was a regular feature in tabloids like the *New York Post* and *Daily News*. These papers were eager to cover his larger-than-life personality, his high-profile real estate deals, and his extravagant lifestyle. Trump understood the power of media exposure and was not shy about courting it. He made himself available to journalists, providing them with colorful quotes, exclusive details about his deals, and even insights into his personal life. This constant stream of attention helped build his reputation as a brash, ambitious developer who was always involved in something big.

Trump's ability to control the narrative around his projects became a crucial component of his branding strategy. Even when faced with challenges, such as financial difficulties or stalled developments, Trump was able to steer media coverage in a positive direction, emphasizing his bold vision and future plans rather than setbacks. He framed himself as a risk-taker, someone willing to pursue grand, audacious ideas. This image resonated with the public, feeding the myth of Trump as a man who never backed down from a challenge.

While Trump initially relied on print media to build his brand, the advent of television provided him with an even larger platform. Television allowed Trump to reach millions of viewers, putting a face and a voice to the name that had become synonymous with luxury real estate. His appearances on talk shows, news programs, and interviews were opportunities to not only promote his latest projects but also to showcase his charismatic, confident persona. He quickly became a fixture on shows like *Larry King Live* and *The Today Show*, where he discussed everything from his business deals to his personal life, ensuring that his name stayed in the spotlight.

Trump's understanding of media extended beyond traditional outlets. In 1987, he published his first book, *The Art of the Deal*, which became an instant bestseller. The book was more than just a business memoir—it was a carefully crafted piece of self-promotion. Written in a conversational, accessible style, *The Art of the Deal* offered readers insights into Trump's philosophy on business and life, painting him as a master negotiator and visionary entrepreneur. The book not only bolstered Trump's reputation as a businessman but also cemented his status as a pop culture figure. It was a key moment in the evolution of the Trump brand, turning him from a New York real estate developer into a national figure.

However, it was reality television that would provide Trump with his most powerful media platform yet. In 2004, *The Apprentice* premiered, and with it, Trump became a household name. The show wasn't just a business competition—it was a showcase for Trump's brand and persona. Each episode featured Trump as the

ultimate authority figure, presiding over a group of aspiring entrepreneurs with his trademark mix of charm, wit, and ruthless decision-making. The now-iconic catchphrase "You're fired" became
synonymous with Trump, reinforcing his image as a no-nonsense,
results-oriented leader.

The Apprentice was more than just a successful TV show—it
was a branding masterstroke. It allowed Trump to reach millions
of viewers each week, many of whom had no prior knowledge
of his real estate ventures but were drawn to his charismatic on-
screen persona. The show painted Trump as a larger-than-life
figure, embodying the principles of success, power, and wealth
that were central to the Trump brand. Through The Apprentice,
Trump's image became accessible to a global audience, and his
brand was strengthened by the perception that he was the ultimate
business expert.

Trump's use of media wasn't limited to traditional formats. As
the internet became an increasingly important platform for communication, Trump embraced new ways to engage with the public. He maintained a constant presence in online news, and later on
social media, where his brash, unfiltered style found a new home.
His ability to generate headlines—whether through provocative
statements, bold business moves, or high-profile feuds—kept him
in the news cycle and ensured that the Trump brand was always
part of the national conversation.

Even as Trump's business ventures evolved, his relationship
with the media remained a cornerstone of his brand-building
strategy. By consistently staying in the public eye, Trump ensured
that his name—and by extension, his brand—remained relevant.
He understood that in the modern business landscape, visibility
was just as important as success. The more people saw and heard
about Trump, the more his brand was reinforced as a symbol of
success and luxury.

In the end, Trump's mastery of media allowed him to cultivate a global brand that transcended real estate and entered the realms of entertainment, politics, and popular culture. His ability to craft and control his narrative in the media helped build a brand that was not only enduring but also adaptable, evolving with the times and expanding into new markets. From tabloid headlines to prime-time television, Donald Trump turned the media into one of his most powerful assets, using it to build a brand that became a global phenomenon.

Expanding the Trump Brand into Hospitality

As Donald Trump continued to grow his real estate empire, it became increasingly clear that his brand was no longer confined to skyscrapers and casinos. His vision was much broader—he wanted to extend the Trump name into a fully integrated lifestyle brand, with a focus on luxury living and high-end experiences. The hospitality industry, with its direct connection to personal comfort and luxury, was a natural fit for Trump's ambitions. By expanding into hotels, resorts, and golf courses, Trump found a new avenue to solidify his brand as a symbol of opulence and exclusivity.

Trump's move into the hotel business began in earnest in the 1980s, with his acquisition and development of several high-profile properties. One of his earliest forays was the purchase of the Plaza Hotel in New York City. The Plaza, already a storied landmark, fit perfectly with Trump's strategy of associating his brand with iconic luxury. In his typically bold style, Trump spared no expense in renovating the property, investing millions to restore the hotel's grandeur while adding his signature touch of extravagance. The Plaza was more than just another hotel for Trump—it was a statement, a way of aligning his brand with the ultimate symbol of high-end hospitality.

However, the true cornerstone of Trump's expansion into hospitality was the development of the Trump International Hotel and Tower brand. Starting with his flagship property on Central Park West in New York, Trump International properties quickly became known for their luxurious accommodations, impeccable service, and prime locations. These hotels weren't just places to stay—they were experiences in themselves, designed to appeal to the world's elite who valued privacy, prestige, and comfort.

Trump's hotels were meticulously designed to embody the key elements of his brand: grandeur, luxury, and exclusivity. From the moment guests entered a Trump hotel, they were immersed in a world of marble, crystal chandeliers, and high-end finishes. Every detail, from the architecture to the service, was carefully crafted to project an image of unrivaled luxury. Trump himself was heavily involved in the design and management of these properties, ensuring that the Trump brand was represented at the highest level of quality. This hands-on approach reinforced the perception that a stay at a Trump hotel was a guarantee of excellence.

One of the most significant expansions of the Trump brand into hospitality came with the development of his golf resorts. Trump saw the potential to combine his love for the game with his branding prowess by creating world-class golf courses and luxury resorts. Trump National Golf Clubs and Trump International Golf Links were established across the United States and in prestigious international locations, each offering pristine golf courses, exclusive clubhouses, and high-end amenities. These resorts weren't just about golf—they were about the experience of being part of an elite, private world that reflected the Trump ethos of luxury and success.

Trump's golf courses became a powerful extension of his brand, particularly as he positioned them in some of the world's most desirable locations, such as Scotland, Ireland, and the

Caribbean. The courses themselves were designed to attract professional golfers, high-net-worth individuals, and international tourists, all of whom associated the Trump name with the finest in leisure and luxury. For Trump, these properties were more than profitable investments; they were symbols of his global reach and ability to create world-class destinations under his brand.

Trump's expansion into the luxury hospitality sector also included residential real estate. Trump-branded residential towers were built in prime locations around the world, from Chicago to Dubai. These properties offered high-end apartments and penthouses, designed to cater to wealthy buyers who valued not just luxury living but also the prestige that came with the Trump name. The Trump Organization marketed these properties as part of an exclusive club, where ownership meant aligning oneself with a brand known for excellence, wealth, and power. Buyers weren't just purchasing a home; they were investing in the Trump lifestyle.

Trump's ability to market his hospitality ventures relied heavily on the strength of his personal brand. Whether it was a hotel in New York or a golf resort in Scotland, the Trump name carried with it the promise of a particular experience—one defined by high standards, luxury amenities, and personalized service. This brand recognition allowed Trump to charge premium prices for rooms, memberships, and real estate, knowing that customers were willing to pay for the privilege of associating with the Trump brand. In many cases, the Trump name itself became the product, as much as the properties he developed.

One of the keys to Trump's success in hospitality was his ability to differentiate his properties from competitors. In a market where luxury hotels and resorts were already abundant, Trump relied on his personal fame and the mystique of his brand to stand out. His properties weren't just marketed as luxurious—they were marketed as "Trump luxurious," a step above the rest, offering experiences that could not be matched by other brands. By tying his personal reputation to his hotels, golf courses, and residential developments, Trump created a brand that was not only synonymous with luxury but also with aspiration. To stay at a Trump hotel, play at a Trump golf course, or live in a Trump residence was to be part of an elite world where success and wealth were celebrated.

As Trump's hospitality empire grew, so did the global recognition of the Trump brand. His hotels and resorts became destinations for celebrities, politicians, and wealthy travelers from around the world. Whether they were staying in New York, Las Vegas, or Dubai, guests were choosing to stay at a Trump property not just for its luxury, but for the association with the man behind the brand. For Donald Trump, the expansion into hospitality was more than just another business venture—it was the ultimate expression of his brand's power and reach, a way to bring the Trump name into the everyday lives of the world's most successful and aspirational individuals.

Licensing the Trump Name Globally

By the mid-1990s, Donald Trump had already established a firm foothold in real estate, hospitality, and entertainment. But the true genius of his branding lay in his ability to extend the Trump name into a wide array of industries beyond those he directly controlled. Recognizing the power of his brand, Trump pursued an aggressive strategy of licensing, allowing third-party developers and companies to use his name on projects and products worldwide. This approach enabled him to grow the Trump empire exponentially, without the need for direct investment or operational oversight, while maintaining a consistent association with luxury and prestige.

Licensing became a major aspect of Trump's business strategy, particularly as the value of his brand continued to rise. Through licensing agreements, developers could pay to use the Trump name on their buildings, with the understanding that it would significantly boost the market value of the project. The Trump brand carried weight, particularly in the realms of high-end real estate and luxury hospitality. Buyers and investors were willing to pay a premium for the assurance that a property bearing the Trump name would embody the qualities of grandeur, exclusivity, and high-end design.

This strategy of licensing allowed Trump to extend his brand's influence far beyond New York City and the United States. Trump-branded buildings began to appear in international cities, from Toronto to Istanbul to Manila, each one capitalizing on the cachet of the Trump name. By associating these properties with his brand, Trump provided an instant aura of luxury, even in markets where he had no physical presence or involvement in the project's development. This global expansion helped cement the Trump name as a symbol of luxury real estate, recognized in nearly every major city in the world.

One of the most striking examples of this strategy was Trump's foray into the luxury condominium market. Trump-branded residential towers began to spring up in locations across the globe, many of which were developed by third-party companies that licensed the Trump name. These developments offered a range of luxury amenities, from private gyms to high-end restaurants, all designed to evoke the same sense of prestige that Trump had cultivated in his U.S. properties. Buyers in markets as diverse as Panama, India, and the Middle East were eager to associate their homes with the Trump brand, viewing it as a status symbol and a guarantee of quality.

Licensing agreements extended well beyond real estate. Trump saw an opportunity to expand his brand into consumer products, leveraging his name to create an array of goods that bore the Trump logo. These ranged from men's fashion lines, such as Trump-branded suits, ties, and accessories, to home furnishings, cologne, and even bottled water. The Trump name became a stamp of approval, signifying that a product was designed for those who aspired to luxury living. Trump understood that consumers were not just buying a product—they were buying a piece of his brand, and with it, the image of success and affluence that came with the Trump lifestyle.

One of the most successful consumer product lines was Trump's venture into high-end home goods. Trump Home, a brand offering luxury furniture and décor, was created in partnership with various manufacturers. The line targeted affluent buyers who wanted to furnish their homes with items that reflected the same elegance and sophistication associated with Trump's properties. Whether it was a plush sofa, a grand chandelier, or sleek dining room furniture, Trump Home products were designed to evoke the lavish interiors found in Trump's hotels and residential developments. Once again, the Trump brand's association with luxury helped these products command premium prices in the marketplace.

Another significant licensing success came in the form of Trump's partnership with major real estate developers in Asia and the Middle East. In these markets, the Trump brand was viewed as a symbol of Western luxury and aspiration. Projects such as Trump Tower Mumbai in India and Trump Towers in Manila capitalized on the prestige of the Trump name to attract wealthy buyers and investors. These developments, though managed and built by local companies, carried the imprimatur of the Trump brand, ensuring that they were marketed as luxury properties on par with the finest developments in New York and other global cities.

Trump's licensing deals were not limited to real estate and consumer goods; he also ventured into entertainment and media. From 2004 to 2015, *The Apprentice* became one of the most successful reality TV shows in history, further bolstering Trump's brand. This gave rise to a series of spin-offs, endorsements, and product partnerships, all of which leveraged the power of Trump's name. The show, which positioned Trump as the ultimate business authority, elevated his public image to new heights, and the association with success and power further enhanced the allure of the Trump brand.

What made Trump's licensing strategy particularly effective was its scalability. By allowing third parties to develop and sell products under the Trump name, Trump could expand his brand globally without the need for direct capital investment or the risks associated with large-scale development projects. He could lend his name to projects and products that fit his brand's ethos while remaining relatively detached from day-to-day operations. This approach enabled the Trump Organization to maintain a wide portfolio of branded properties and products without becoming overstretched financially.

Of course, there were inherent risks in this strategy. By allowing third parties to use his name, Trump had to trust that these developers and manufacturers would uphold the quality and luxury standards associated with his brand. While most licensing deals were successful, there were instances where projects fell short of expectations, leading to legal battles and brand reputation concerns. However, Trump's meticulous approach to selecting partners and his insistence on maintaining control over the use of his name helped mitigate these risks and preserved the brand's integrity.

Ultimately, Donald Trump's ability to transform his name into a global brand through licensing was a testament to his understanding of the power of image. By strategically leveraging the Trump name across industries and borders, he turned what began as a family real estate business into an empire that spanned continents and sectors. The Trump brand became more than a symbol of real estate success; it became synonymous with luxury, power, and aspiration, touching nearly every facet of modern life, from where people lived to what they wore. Through licensing, Donald Trump was able to transform his business ventures into a global brand empire that would endure, even as the world of real estate continued to evolve.

| 8 |

Chapter 8: Trump Hotels and Resorts

The Vision Behind Trump Hotels

Donald Trump's foray into the hotel business was not just an extension of his real estate empire; it was the realization of a carefully crafted vision to create a global luxury brand synonymous with opulence, exclusivity, and exceptional service. Trump understood early on that the hotel industry was about more than providing rooms for guests—it was about selling an experience, a lifestyle that catered to the wealthy elite who expected the very best. His entry into hospitality was fueled by the belief that his name, already synonymous with luxury real estate, could offer something unique in a competitive market: the promise of "the Trump standard."

From the outset, Trump's strategy for his hotels and resorts was simple yet ambitious. He wanted to provide the ultimate luxury experience, one that combined lavish amenities, impeccable service, and architectural grandeur in prime locations. Trump had always believed that success in business was tied to creating value that exceeded expectations, and in the hospitality industry, this meant offering guests something they couldn't find anywhere else—a blend of personal attention and grandiosity that would make every stay feel extraordinary.

Trump's vision for his hotel business was rooted in his larger philosophy of branding. Just as he had done with his real estate projects, Trump understood the power of attaching his name to a luxury product. He believed that when people saw the Trump name, they associated it with the highest level of quality, luxury, and prestige. This association was not by accident but by design. Over the years, Trump had built his brand through high-profile developments, media appearances, and a reputation for creating iconic, luxurious spaces. With this established foundation, his move into hotels felt like a natural progression.

In interviews and public appearances, Trump frequently emphasized that the Trump Hotels brand would represent "the best of the best." This slogan wasn't just a marketing line—it was a guiding principle. Trump was personally involved in every aspect of the hotel's development, from selecting the locations to approving design choices. He sought to differentiate his hotels from competitors by ensuring that every detail, no matter how small, was up to his exacting standards. Whether it was the thread count of the sheets or the marble used in the lobbies, Trump was committed to creating an environment that embodied luxury at every turn.

Another key element of Trump's vision was his belief in the power of location. In real estate, Trump had always focused on securing prime locations, and he brought the same focus to his hotels. He understood that the success of a hotel depended not only on the quality of the accommodations but also on its proximity to landmarks, business centers, and other attractions that would draw affluent travelers. Trump International Hotel & Tower in New York, for example, was strategically located on Central Park West, providing guests with stunning views of the park and easy access to the city's most iconic attractions.

Trump's vision for his hotels also extended to the type of experience he wanted to provide. Unlike many other luxury hotel brands, which focused primarily on corporate travelers or vacationers, Trump Hotels were designed to cater to a broader spectrum of high-net-worth individuals. Business moguls, celebrities, and wealthy families were all part of Trump's target demographic, and he ensured that his hotels offered amenities tailored to their specific needs. From state-of-the-art business centers to world-class spas, Trump's properties were designed to make every guest feel like a VIP.

One of the defining features of Trump's vision was his emphasis on personalized service. Trump believed that true luxury wasn't just about lavish surroundings—it was about how guests were treated. He wanted every guest to feel as though they were staying in a home away from home, albeit one with every possible comfort and indulgence. His hotels were staffed with employees trained to anticipate guests' needs, from personalized check-ins to custom itineraries for their stays. This level of attention to detail was central to Trump's philosophy of creating a "five-star" experience, not just in terms of physical amenities but in the overall feeling of being pampered and valued.

Moreover, Trump wasn't content to just develop luxury hotels; he wanted to create iconic properties that would stand as symbols of his brand. His vision for Trump Hotels was about more than profitability—it was about legacy. He viewed each hotel as a statement piece, a monument to the Trump brand that would endure for generations. Trump saw his hotels as modern-day palaces, where the world's elite could come to experience the very best that life had to offer.

In many ways, Trump's entry into the hotel business reflected his broader entrepreneurial ethos: go big, go bold, and create something that no one else can match. He didn't just want to compete in the luxury hotel space—he wanted to dominate it. And while other hotel chains focused on expanding through volume and scale, Trump's strategy was more selective. He would rather open fewer properties that were truly exceptional than flood the market with hotels that diluted the prestige of his brand.

In the years that followed, Trump's vision for his hotel empire would take shape, with properties that spanned the globe, each one embodying the key elements that defined his brand: luxury, exclusivity, and an unwavering commitment to excellence. From New York to Las Vegas, from Toronto to Dubai, Trump Hotels became synonymous with the kind of high-end experience that appealed to the world's wealthiest and most discerning travelers. Through his vision, Donald Trump had successfully transformed the Trump name into a global symbol of luxury hospitality.

Flagship Properties and Global Expansion

As Donald Trump expanded his real estate ventures into the hotel industry, his focus was on creating flagship properties that would not only embody his vision of luxury but also serve as iconic symbols of the Trump brand. The development of Trump International Hotel & Tower in New York City marked the beginning of this new chapter in Trump's empire. Located on Central Park West, this hotel would set the standard for what guests could expect from a Trump-branded property, establishing a benchmark for future developments both in the U.S. and around the globe.

The decision to build Trump International Hotel & Tower in New York was a strategic one. Trump understood the importance of location in the hospitality industry, and no location was more prestigious than Central Park West. The property, situated in the heart of Manhattan, provided unparalleled views of Central Park, while offering easy access to some of the city's most important cultural landmarks, including Lincoln Center, the Museum of Modern Art, and Fifth Avenue. This prime location ensured that Trump's hotel would attract both tourists and business travelers seeking luxury accommodations in one of the most sought-after neighborhoods in the world.

Trump International Hotel & Tower was not just a hotel, but a mixed-use development that included residential units. This dual-purpose design became a hallmark of many of Trump's later projects. By combining luxury residences with five-star hotel services, Trump was able to create a unique product that appealed to high-net-worth individuals looking for a combination of privacy, exclusivity, and the amenities of a luxury hotel. Residents and guests alike could enjoy the best of both worlds—living in a private apartment while having access to a concierge, in-room dining, spa services, and more.

The success of Trump International Hotel & Tower New York laid the foundation for Trump's hotel expansion strategy. Having proven that his vision of luxury hospitality could compete in one of the world's most competitive markets, Trump set his sights on other major cities, both domestically and internationally. Chicago, Las Vegas, and Toronto became key targets for expansion, each offering unique opportunities to build landmark properties that would carry the Trump name to new heights.

Trump International Hotel & Tower Chicago was one of the most ambitious projects in Trump's portfolio. The 92-story skyscraper, located along the Chicago River, was not only one of the tallest buildings in the city but also one of the most luxurious. Designed by renowned architect Adrian Smith, the tower featured sleek, modern lines and a reflective glass exterior that captured the city's skyline in breathtaking detail. Inside, guests and residents were treated to the kind of extravagance that had become synonymous with the Trump brand—spacious suites, lavishly appointed interiors, and world-class amenities, including a Michelin-starred restaurant and a 23,000-square-foot spa.

Like his New York property, the Chicago development was a mixed-use building, combining luxury residences with a five-star hotel. This model allowed Trump to appeal to both the city's elite and visitors seeking a premium experience. The hotel's proximity to Chicago's business district and shopping areas made it a popular choice for corporate travelers, while its unrivaled views of Lake Michigan and the Chicago River attracted tourists from around the world.

In Las Vegas, Trump took a different approach. The Trump International Hotel Las Vegas, unlike many of the city's famous resorts, did not feature a casino. This was a deliberate decision on Trump's part, as he wanted to offer a distinct alternative to the typical Las Vegas experience. Instead of the noisy, bustling atmosphere associated with casino hotels, Trump's Las Vegas property focused entirely on luxury and serenity. The hotel catered to visitors who wanted the glamour of Las Vegas without the crowds and chaos of the Strip. With its gold-tinted glass tower rising high above the city, the Trump International Hotel Las Vegas became a beacon of understated elegance in a city known for its excess.

While Trump's domestic hotel expansion was impressive, his global ambitions were just as significant. Recognizing the growing demand for luxury accommodations in international markets, Trump sought to take his brand to some of the world's most important cities. One of his first major international ventures was Trump International Hotel & Tower Toronto, a development that brought Trump's signature luxury to Canada's largest city. Located in the heart of Toronto's financial district, the hotel catered to business travelers and tourists alike, offering stunning views of Lake Ontario and the downtown skyline. Like his other properties, the Toronto development featured a combination of hotel rooms and residences, with an emphasis on premium service and personalized attention.

Trump's expansion into international markets was driven by a desire to capitalize on the growing global demand for luxury hospitality. Cities like Toronto, Vancouver, and Panama City represented opportunities to introduce the Trump brand to new audiences, particularly in regions where high-net-worth individuals were seeking exclusive, high-end accommodations. The Trump Hotels brand, with its reputation for unparalleled service and opulent design, was well-positioned to attract these affluent travelers.

In addition to North America, Trump Hotels began to make inroads into other international markets. The brand's expansion into Asia, with developments in Manila and Mumbai, signaled Trump's intention to grow his hotel empire in regions with rapidly expanding economies and a growing class of luxury consumers. Trump Tower Manila, for example, became one of the most sought-after addresses in the Philippines, combining Trump's signature luxury with the city's vibrant culture and growing economy.

Trump's global expansion was not without its challenges. Entering new markets required navigating complex regulatory environments, working with local developers, and adapting to cultural differences. However, Trump's ability to partner with experienced local teams helped mitigate these risks. His strategy of licensing the Trump name to third-party developers also allowed him to expand his brand with minimal financial exposure, while still maintaining control over the quality and standards of the properties.

Ultimately, the flagship properties that Trump developed and licensed globally helped establish the Trump Hotels brand as a major player in the luxury hospitality industry. From New York to Las Vegas to international markets, each property carried the same promise of excellence, exclusivity, and personalized service.

Trump's hotels became synonymous with the kind of luxury experience that high-end travelers sought, further cementing his reputation as a branding genius in the world of real estate and hospitality.

The Trump Standard: Architecture and Design

One of the most striking aspects of Donald Trump's approach to the hotel industry was his unwavering focus on architecture and design. For Trump, a hotel was not merely a place to stay; it was an experience shaped as much by its physical presence as by the service it offered. In his vision, the structure itself had to be a statement—an unmistakable declaration of luxury, power, and exclusivity. Every Trump hotel was a reflection of this vision, with an emphasis on bold architecture and meticulous interior design that set his properties apart from the competition.

Trump had always believed that great architecture was essential to creating iconic buildings that would stand the test of time. This belief was evident in his earlier real estate ventures, such as Trump Tower in New York City, but when it came to his hotels, he pushed his architectural ambitions even further. For each new project, Trump sought out some of the world's top architects and designers, demanding that they bring his vision of opulence to life while also ensuring that the structures would have a unique aesthetic that would distinguish them from anything else in the market.

In Trump's view, luxury was about more than just expensive materials and large spaces—it was about creating an emotional response. He wanted his hotels to evoke awe from the moment a guest arrived, which meant that every detail, both inside and out, had to be carefully curated to achieve that effect. The exterior of a Trump hotel was designed to impress, often featuring soaring towers of glass and steel, while the interiors were crafted to envelop guests in a world of elegance, comfort, and refinement.

Take, for example, the design of Trump International Hotel & Tower in Chicago. Standing at 1,389 feet tall, this skyscraper was one of the tallest in the world at the time of its completion. Trump wanted a building that would be as iconic as the Willis Tower (formerly known as the Sears Tower), but with a more modern and luxurious feel. The architect, Adrian Smith, designed the building with a reflective glass facade that shimmered in the sunlight and mirrored the Chicago River below. Inside, the hotel boasted marble-clad lobbies, custom-designed furniture, and expansive suites that featured floor-to-ceiling windows, offering breathtaking views of the city skyline and Lake Michigan.

Trump's hands-on involvement in the design process extended to the interiors of his hotels as well. He was known to personally approve every detail, from the choice of chandeliers to the color scheme of the rooms. Luxury, in Trump's mind, was about creating a sensory experience—guests should feel the opulence in every touch, whether it was the weight of a doorknob, the smoothness of marble underfoot, or the softness of a cashmere throw draped over a king-sized bed.

This attention to detail was not limited to the rooms themselves. Trump believed that every space within the hotel had to contribute to the overall experience of luxury. Public spaces like the lobby, restaurants, and spas were designed to exude a sense of grandeur. In Trump's New York hotel, for instance, the lobby featured polished brass, rich wood paneling, and ornate chandeliers that gave the space a feeling of timeless elegance. The design was meant to evoke the opulence of a bygone era, while still offering the modern amenities that guests of a five-star hotel expected.

Another hallmark of Trump's approach to architecture and design was his insistence on using only the finest materials. Trump believed that guests would immediately notice the difference between standard luxury and the true extravagance that came from using top-tier materials. He spared no expense when it came to sourcing rare marbles, imported woods, and custom-made fixtures. In many of his properties, even the smallest details, such as the bathroom tiles or the hardware on doors, were made from the highest quality materials, often imported from Europe or other parts of the world known for craftsmanship and luxury goods.

Trump's obsession with quality extended to the amenities in his hotels. Spas were often designed to rival those found in the most exclusive resorts, featuring marble treatment rooms, infinity pools, and saunas with panoramic views of the city or ocean. Fitness centers were equipped with the latest high-tech machines, and Trump often worked with celebrity chefs to ensure that the hotel restaurants were among the best in their cities. Every aspect of the guest's stay was designed to reinforce the idea that they were experiencing the height of luxury.

One of the more unique elements of Trump's approach to hotel design was his focus on creating properties that were timeless yet modern. He didn't want his hotels to feel like they belonged to a particular era; instead, he aimed for a balance of classic elegance and contemporary style. This was evident in the way his hotels blended traditional architectural elements—like the use of limestone and bronze—with sleek, modern touches such as glass facades and state-of-the-art technology. The result was a design that felt both familiar and innovative, appealing to guests who appreciated old-world charm as well as those who valued cutting-edge sophistication.

Despite his desire for luxury, Trump also understood that a hotel had to be functional and comfortable. Guest rooms were designed with both aesthetics and practicality in mind. They were spacious, with large windows that maximized natural light, and often featured separate living areas, walk-in closets, and oversized bathrooms. Trump wanted guests to feel as though they were staying in their own private residence, with all the conveniences and luxuries that entailed.

Ultimately, Trump's emphasis on architecture and design played a critical role in defining the Trump Hotels brand. By creating properties that were as visually stunning as they were luxurious, Trump was able to distinguish his hotels from the competition and attract guests who were seeking more than just a place to sleep—they were looking for an experience. Whether staying in New York, Chicago, or Las Vegas, guests knew that a Trump hotel would offer not only the finest service but also a setting that was both grand and welcoming. It was this combination of architectural boldness and interior refinement that made Trump Hotels a standout in the global luxury market, embodying the Trump standard that guests came to expect.

Building the Trump Brand Through Celebrity and Media

One of Donald Trump's most powerful tools in building his hotel empire was his ability to leverage celebrity status and media presence to promote the Trump brand. Long before entering politics, Trump was a household name, and he knew how to use that visibility to his advantage in the business world. While many hotel chains relied solely on reputation, reviews, or advertising campaigns to generate interest, Trump had a unique edge—he was the face of his own brand, and his larger-than-life personality helped create buzz and excitement around every new venture.

Trump's relationship with the media began early in his career. From the late 1970s onward, Trump became a regular feature in New York tabloids and national publications, both for his real estate accomplishments and his personal life. Whether he was announcing a new skyscraper, attending high-profile events, or making headlines with his bold statements, Trump understood the importance of keeping his name in the spotlight. This media exposure not only elevated Trump's personal profile but also added prestige to the projects he was working on. When Trump built a new hotel, it wasn't just another real estate development—it was a Trump development, with all the glamour and drama that implied.

As his hotel ventures expanded, Trump became even more adept at turning media attention into a marketing tool. One of the key moments in this strategy was the release of his best-selling book, *The Art of the Deal*, in 1987. The book not only chronicled his rise in the business world but also painted a picture of Trump as the ultimate dealmaker—someone who could navigate complex negotiations, take risks, and come out on top. *The Art of the Deal* helped solidify Trump's image as a savvy businessman and further associated his name with success, power, and luxury. The book's success boosted his profile and increased interest in his ventures, including his hotels. Potential guests didn't just see Trump's properties as places to stay—they saw them as extensions of Trump's personality and success.

But it wasn't just traditional media that helped Trump expand his hotel empire. In the early 2000s, Trump found a new platform to showcase his business acumen: reality television. In 2004, he launched *The Apprentice*, a show in which contestants competed for a job within Trump's organization. The show was an instant hit, with millions tuning in each week to watch Trump critique contestants and deliver his famous "You're fired" catchphrase. The success of *The Apprentice* was transformative for the Trump brand. Overnight, Trump became not only a media personality but also a symbol of business success, viewed by millions of Americans as the ultimate judge of talent and leadership.

The Apprentice was more than just entertainment—it was a marketing platform for Trump's businesses, including his hotels. Throughout the series, Trump frequently featured his properties, using them as the backdrop for key challenges or as locations for glamorous events. By showcasing his hotels on a national stage, Trump was able to reach an audience that might not have been familiar with the Trump Hotels brand. Viewers of *The Apprentice* got a firsthand look at the luxurious interiors of Trump Tower, Trump International Hotel, and other properties, reinforcing the image of Trump's hotels as premier destinations for those seeking the best of the best.

In addition to the exposure generated by the show itself, Trump's role as a television personality elevated his profile to new heights. He became a ubiquitous figure in pop culture, making guest appearances on talk shows, being parodied on *Saturday Night Live*, and even hosting prestigious events at his hotels. This level of visibility was unmatched by other hoteliers, who rarely enjoyed the same kind of personal brand recognition. For Trump, every television appearance, interview, or media mention was an opportunity to promote his hotels and the larger Trump brand.

Trump's use of celebrity endorsements also played a role in building the prestige of his hotel empire. High-profile events at Trump properties, whether it was the Miss Universe pageant (which he co-owned for several years) or celebrity-studded galas, helped create an aura of exclusivity and excitement around his hotels. Guests didn't just want to stay at a Trump hotel—they wanted to be part of the glamorous, celebrity-filled world that Trump had cultivated through his media presence. The association with fame and luxury created a powerful draw for wealthy travelers, making Trump hotels a preferred destination for the elite.

Moreover, Trump's hotels became a natural choice for movie shoots, television scenes, and high-profile interviews. The grandeur of his properties made them ideal locations for productions seeking to portray opulence, wealth, and success. Films like *Home Alone 2: Lost in New York* and shows like *Gossip Girl* featured scenes shot at Trump properties, further ingraining these hotels in popular culture. Trump was able to monetize his celebrity status, while also using it as a way to constantly promote the image of his hotels as iconic symbols of luxury.

Trump's strategic use of media and celebrity endorsements was not limited to the United States. As his hotel empire expanded globally, so did his media presence. Trump properties hosted events for world leaders, celebrities, and international business elites. The Trump name became synonymous with luxury and exclusivity worldwide, and each hotel opening was treated as a high-profile media event. From ribbon-cutting ceremonies with top global figures to lavish launch parties, Trump ensured that the world was watching every time a new Trump hotel opened its doors.

In summary, Donald Trump's understanding of media and celebrity was one of the key factors in the success of his hotel empire. By making himself the face of his brand and utilizing television, books, and high-profile events to generate constant attention, Trump was able to turn his properties into more than just luxury hotels—they became symbols of his personal success and the aspirational lifestyle associated with the Trump name. Through strategic media engagement, Trump transformed his hotels into destinations that were as much about the experience of staying in a Trump-branded property as they were about the physical accommodations themselves.

Expanding Trump Hotels to Global Luxury Destinations

As Donald Trump's hotel empire grew, so did his ambition to expand the Trump brand beyond the United States. He recognized that to truly establish his company as a global force in the luxury hotel market, he would need to take his brand to some of the most exclusive and desirable destinations around the world. Trump's strategy was not just about building hotels—it was about building iconic properties in locations that would enhance the prestige of the Trump name, from international financial hubs to exotic vacation spots. Expanding globally wasn't merely an aspiration for Trump; it was a key to cementing the Trump brand as synonymous with luxury, grandeur, and international prominence.

One of the first significant steps in this global expansion was Trump International Hotel & Tower in Toronto, Canada, which opened in 2012. This towering structure, rising 65 stories above the city, was designed to be one of the most luxurious hotels and residences in Canada's financial capital. For Trump, the location was perfect—Toronto was a growing city with a booming economy, and he saw an opportunity to position the Trump brand as a leader in the market for both high-end travelers and wealthy local residents seeking luxury condos. The property featured all the hallmarks of a Trump hotel, including opulent suites, fine dining, and a state-of-the-art spa, but it also incorporated elements that reflected Toronto's cosmopolitan identity, blending local design with Trump's signature aesthetic of lavish comfort.

While Toronto marked a significant milestone, Trump's ambitions didn't stop at North America. The Trump Hotel Collection set its sights on Europe and the Middle East, regions where high-end luxury hotels were in great demand from global travelers. One of the most notable projects was Trump International Golf Links & Hotel in Doonbeg, Ireland. Acquired by Trump in 2014, the Doonbeg property wasn't just a hotel—it was a premier golf destination set against the backdrop of the rugged Irish coastline. Trump saw an opportunity to combine his passion for golf with the luxury hotel experience, offering a unique destination for both golfers and those seeking a peaceful retreat in one of Ireland's most picturesque landscapes.

The Doonbeg property highlighted another aspect of Trump's global strategy—his ability to tap into the niche market of luxury golf resorts. Trump International Golf Links in Scotland was another project that showcased this approach. Built on the coast of Aberdeenshire, this world-class golf course and accompanying hotel became an immediate draw for international golfers. Trump's reputation in the golf world, combined with his attention to detail in both course design and hotel amenities, helped cement the Trump name as not only a major player in luxury hotels but also in the world of high-end golf tourism.

Trump's global hotel expansion wasn't confined to just leisure destinations; he also targeted key financial hubs where demand for luxury accommodations was high. Trump International Hotel & Tower in Vancouver, which opened in 2017, exemplified this strategy. The Vancouver property stood as a sleek, ultra-modern building in the heart of the city, offering travelers not only the lavishness expected from a Trump hotel but also proximity to Vancouver's bustling business district. The hotel featured expansive views of the city and mountains, exquisite dining options, and residences designed for the ultra-wealthy. By placing his hotels in major global cities, Trump was able to appeal to both business travelers and high-net-worth individuals, furthering his goal of making the Trump brand a global symbol of success.

Another standout in Trump's global portfolio was Trump International Hotel in Dubai, part of the massive luxury development known as DAMAC Hills. Dubai, known for its opulence and grandeur, was a natural fit for Trump's brand, and this property was a collaboration with Dubai-based real estate giant DAMAC Properties. The Dubai hotel combined Trump's aesthetic of luxury with the Middle Eastern city's love for extravagant design, creating a property that appealed to both local elites and international tourists. The partnership with DAMAC also signaled Trump's ability to work with international developers to extend his brand's reach into highly competitive and prestigious markets.

Trump's expansion into global markets wasn't just about building hotels; it was about creating a presence in cities and regions where the Trump name could add a unique value to the local hospitality market. He carefully selected locations where there was a demand for ultra-luxury accommodations, while also ensuring that the properties would stand out as architectural and experiential landmarks. Each hotel in the Trump International portfolio was designed to reflect not just the luxury Trump was known for, but also the specific culture and environment of its location, whether it was the beaches of Ireland, the financial districts of Canada, or the opulent skyline of Dubai.

The global expansion of Trump Hotels wasn't without challenges, especially as international markets faced fluctuations in economic conditions, local regulations, and political climates. However, Trump's approach to risk management in his business, as well as his ability to adapt to different market needs, allowed him to navigate these challenges effectively. He worked with local partners and developers to ensure that each project would be both a financial success and a statement of Trump's commitment to maintaining his brand's global prominence. Even in regions where the Trump brand faced resistance, such as political opposition or skepticism, Trump's focus remained on the core values of luxury, exclusivity, and world-class service.

In summary, the global expansion of Trump Hotels marked a new chapter in Donald Trump's business career, one that saw him take his brand to some of the most prestigious and competitive hospitality markets in the world. His strategy of selecting prime locations, incorporating local culture while maintaining the Trump standard of opulence, and leveraging his own celebrity status helped create a global network of hotels that catered to the elite. Whether in the financial hubs of North America, the golf resorts of Europe, or the glittering cities of the Middle East, Trump's hotels became synonymous with the pinnacle of luxury, making the Trump name a permanent fixture in the world of international high-end hospitality.

| 9 |

Chapter 9: The Apprentice and Media Dominance

The Birth of The Apprentice and Trump's Vision

By the early 2000s, Donald Trump was already a well-known figure in the worlds of real estate and business, but his public persona was still largely tied to his success as a New York City developer. That all changed with *The Apprentice*, the reality television show that would not only catapult him to global stardom but also redefine his image as a business leader. The creation of *The Apprentice* was a pivotal moment in Trump's career—one where his instinct for media and branding intersected perfectly with the entertainment world's growing appetite for reality TV.

The idea for *The Apprentice* was born out of a collaboration between Trump and reality TV producer Mark Burnett. Burnett was already a rising star in the world of television, having created *Survivor*, one of the most successful reality shows in history. Burnett recognized that Trump's larger-than-life persona and business reputation could be harnessed for a new kind of reality show—one that would combine the drama of competition with the world of high-stakes business. Together, they conceived of a show where aspiring entrepreneurs would compete for the chance to work for Trump, battling through a series of business-related challenges while being judged by Trump and his team.

For Trump, the show was an opportunity to showcase not only his business acumen but also his personality. He wanted *The Apprentice* to serve as a reflection of the way he conducted business—focused, results-oriented, and unapologetically tough. The show would give him a platform to present himself as the ultimate dealmaker, someone who understood what it took to succeed in the cutthroat world of business. It was important to Trump that the show wasn't just entertainment; it needed to convey the seriousness and complexity of running a multi-billion-dollar enterprise. He envisioned *The Apprentice* as a way to impart lessons on leadership, negotiation, and strategy, using real-world scenarios drawn from his own business experience.

The timing of *The Apprentice* could not have been more fortuitous. In the early 2000s, reality television was exploding in popularity, with audiences eager for shows that blended real-life drama with competition. Shows like *Survivor* and *Big Brother* had already paved the way, but there was still an untapped market for reality programming that focused on business and professional success. Trump saw this as a perfect fit for his brand. He was already a well-known figure in the world of real estate, but *The Apprentice* would allow him to reach an entirely new audience—one that was not only interested in business but also fascinated by the persona of a self-made billionaire.

The format of *The Apprentice* was designed to reflect Trump's own business philosophy. Contestants would compete in teams on various business tasks, from selling products to creating marketing campaigns, with each task designed to test their entrepreneurial skills. At the end of each episode, Trump would meet with the losing team in the iconic boardroom, where one contestant would be fired. The boardroom scenes, in particular, became the heart of the show, with Trump's no-nonsense approach and direct feedback creating intense drama. His famous catchphrase, "You're fired," would soon become a cultural phenomenon, embodying Trump's ruthless approach to decision-making and his belief in accountability.

While Mark Burnett's production expertise played a critical role in shaping the show's format, it was Trump's vision that defined its tone and message. Trump insisted that *The Apprentice* should be more than just a game show—it needed to convey real business lessons. He wanted to give viewers insight into what it took to make tough decisions, negotiate high-stakes deals, and lead a successful enterprise. In many ways, *The Apprentice* was an extension of Trump's earlier work with his book *The Art of the Deal*—a public showcase of his philosophy on business and success.

In addition to highlighting Trump's business prowess, the show was also designed to promote the Trump brand. Throughout the series, Trump's properties, from Trump Tower to his luxury hotels, served as the backdrop for the contestants' challenges, reinforcing the image of Trump as a master of the real estate world. Each episode featured scenes of contestants working in Trump's offices or staying in his hotels, subtly promoting the Trump lifestyle—one of luxury, power, and prestige. This not only elevated the show's production value but also created a seamless integration between Trump's media presence and his business ventures.

The launch of *The Apprentice* in 2004 marked the beginning of a new era for Donald Trump. It allowed him to step out from behind the boardroom doors and into the living rooms of millions of Americans, where he became a mentor, a teacher, and, for many, a symbol of success. The show gave Trump a platform to redefine himself, not just as a businessman but as a media personality with a direct line to the public. It was the perfect fusion of his business empire and his growing public persona, setting the stage for a new phase of his career that would have profound implications for both his brand and his future.

In the end, *The Apprentice* wasn't just a television show—it was a statement. It was a declaration of Trump's belief in the power of ambition, competition, and relentless drive. And for Trump, it was a way to bring his business philosophy into the mainstream, using the platform of reality TV to educate and inspire, while simultaneously solidifying his own status as America's most famous entrepreneur.

The Impact of The Apprentice on Trump's Public Image

The success of *The Apprentice* was nothing short of a cultural phenomenon, and its impact on Donald Trump's public image was transformative. Before the show, Trump was known primarily within the realms of real estate and high society, especially in New York. While he had made headlines for his business deals, lavish lifestyle, and occasional controversies, his image was largely that of a wealthy businessman working behind the scenes of skyscrapers and casinos. *The Apprentice* catapulted him into an entirely different realm of fame, turning him into a television star and a recognizable face in millions of households across the country and around the world.

The immediate success of *The Apprentice* surprised even seasoned television producers. Premiering in January 2004, the show quickly became one of NBC's highest-rated programs. Audiences were captivated by the drama of the weekly eliminations, the fierce competition among the contestants, and most of all, Donald Trump's commanding presence as the host and central figure of the show. Trump's persona on the show—confident, decisive, and brutally honest—became a defining aspect of his public identity. He wasn't just a businessman anymore; he was now the personification of American success, a self-made billionaire who represented the American Dream in its most glamorous form.

What set *The Apprentice* apart from other reality shows was the way it portrayed Trump. While other programs focused on personal drama and interpersonal conflict, *The Apprentice* framed Trump as the ultimate judge of business ability. Week after week, viewers saw him sitting at the head of the boardroom table, coolly evaluating the contestants' performances and dispensing his sharp judgments. His catchphrase, "You're fired," became an instant hit and entered the lexicon of popular culture. It wasn't just a line from a TV show—it was a symbol of Trump's no-nonsense approach to business and leadership.

For many viewers, *The Apprentice* presented Trump as an aspirational figure. The show's premise—a competition for a high-level job in the Trump Organization—painted him as a mentor and a gatekeeper to success. Contestants competed not just for a paycheck, but for the opportunity to work for Trump and learn from his expertise. This positioning elevated Trump from a mere businessman to a sort of guru of entrepreneurial success. He became a symbol of what could be achieved through hard work, intelligence, and a bit of ruthlessness. To millions of viewers, Trump was no longer just a real estate tycoon; he was someone to emulate, someone who held the keys to the secrets of wealth and power.

The boardroom scenes in *The Apprentice* were crucial in shaping this new image. Trump's role as the ultimate authority figure allowed him to showcase the traits he believed were necessary for success: decisiveness, confidence, and an unwavering belief in one's vision. These scenes were often filled with tension, as Trump delivered sharp critiques of the contestants' business strategies.

But they also showed a more strategic side of Trump—the businessman who understood what it took to make deals, manage teams, and stay ahead of the competition. His charisma and presence in the boardroom scenes solidified his image as a powerful figure, not just in business, but in life.

Another key aspect of *The Apprentice*'s impact on Trump's image was its ability to make him relatable to a broader audience. Prior to the show, Trump's wealth and lifestyle made him seem distant, almost unapproachable. His name was synonymous with luxury—Trump Tower, Mar-a-Lago, and his fleet of private jets—but these symbols of wealth often made him seem larger-than-life. However, *The Apprentice* humanized Trump to some extent, allowing viewers to see him in action, giving advice, and even occasionally showing moments of humor. While he was still portrayed as an ultra-wealthy businessman, the show's format brought him into people's living rooms in a way that made him more accessible. The audience saw him as someone who had achieved immense success but was willing to share his knowledge and expertise with those striving to follow in his footsteps.

The Apprentice also gave Trump the opportunity to control how he was portrayed in the media. Unlike traditional news coverage or interviews, the show allowed Trump to shape his own narrative. He was in charge—both literally and figuratively—and that control helped him craft an image of himself as the ultimate businessman. He was able to present himself exactly as he wanted to be seen: successful, authoritative, and always in command. This level of control over his public image would prove invaluable in the years to come, as Trump continued to leverage his media presence for personal and professional gain.

Perhaps most importantly, *The Apprentice* expanded Trump's audience far beyond the world of business. Prior to the show, his public image was largely confined to the business elite, New York social circles, and occasional tabloid headlines. *The Apprentice* introduced Trump to a wider demographic, including middle America, younger viewers, and people who had little knowledge of his real estate ventures. The show's broad appeal helped transform Trump into a national figure, and his name became known in households that had never followed his business career. He was no longer just a real estate mogul—he was a television personality, an entertainer, and a cultural icon.

In summary, *The Apprentice* had a profound impact on Donald Trump's public image, turning him from a relatively niche business figure into a global media personality. The show gave him an unprecedented platform to showcase his leadership style, business expertise, and larger-than-life persona, all while positioning him as the epitome of American success. It was this transformation—from businessman to celebrity—that set the stage for Trump's later ventures, both in business and in politics. *The Apprentice* made Donald Trump a household name and, in many ways, laid the foundation for his future in the public eye.

Leveraging Media Power to Expand the Trump Brand

As *The Apprentice* soared in popularity, Donald Trump saw an unprecedented opportunity to leverage his newfound media presence to further expand the Trump brand. What had once been largely confined to the realm of high-end real estate in Manhattan was now poised to become a global empire, reaching far beyond the skyline of New York City. Trump understood the power of visibility, and *The Apprentice* gave him a stage to reach millions of people in a way he had never been able to before. With his larger-than-life persona now ingrained in popular culture, Trump set about expanding his empire through strategic branding and business ventures that capitalized on his heightened visibility.

At the core of Trump's strategy was his understanding that *The Apprentice* wasn't just a television show—it was a platform to showcase his lifestyle, his businesses, and his personal brand. Each episode was a masterclass in self-promotion. The show featured frequent shots of Trump's properties, including Trump Tower, his golf courses, and his luxury hotels. These visuals were more than just set dressing; they were part of Trump's ongoing effort to market his real estate holdings and related businesses as extensions of the "Trump lifestyle"—luxurious, exclusive, and always aspirational. By associating his properties with the high-stakes drama of *The Apprentice*, Trump seamlessly integrated his personal brand into every aspect of the show.

Beyond just real estate, Trump began to expand into other industries that could benefit from his amplified public profile. He recognized that his name had become a valuable asset in itself—a symbol of success, wealth, and ambition. In this new era, the Trump name could be licensed and used to market products and services far beyond his core businesses. Trump began to enter into partnerships that allowed him to lend his name to everything from bottled water and steaks to men's clothing and home furnishings. For Trump, this was a way to expand his brand into markets he had never before tapped, while minimizing the risks traditionally associated with new business ventures. By licensing his name, Trump could make substantial profits without directly managing the day-to-day operations of these products.

The Trump brand was carefully crafted to represent a certain type of wealth and power, and *The Apprentice* helped reinforce that image. By using the show as a platform to promote his luxury hotels, resorts, and golf courses, Trump was able to position these ventures as destinations for those who aspired to the same level of success he embodied on-screen. The show's exposure gave these properties a kind of cachet that traditional marketing campaigns could never achieve. Now, when people stayed at a Trump Hotel or played a round of golf at one of his courses, they weren't just customers—they were participants in the Trump lifestyle, one that was built around opulence, exclusivity, and success.

One of the key ways Trump expanded his brand during this time was through the launch of Trump University in 2005. Trump University was marketed as an educational institution where aspiring entrepreneurs could learn the secrets of Trump's business success. Using *The Apprentice* as a form of credibility, Trump University promised to teach students how to excel in real estate, investment, and personal development, all based on the lessons and principles that had made Trump successful. The school's motto—"Learn from the Master"—was designed to capitalize on Trump's reputation as a business authority, which had been reinforced by his role on *The Apprentice*. While the institution was eventually embroiled in legal controversies, at the time, it was another extension of Trump's media-fueled empire, showing how the Trump name could be applied to nearly any business venture.

In addition to physical products and services, Trump also began to expand his presence in the entertainment world. Recognizing the power of media to shape public perception, he made frequent appearances on talk shows, late-night programs, and interviews, ensuring that his name and face remained in the public consciousness. Trump was a regular guest on shows like *The Late Show with David Letterman*, *Larry King Live*, and *The View*, where he used each appearance to reinforce his image as a successful, no-nonsense businessman. These appearances often revolved around Trump's opinions on current events, business, and his role on *The Apprentice*, further embedding his persona as a savvy, media-savvy entrepreneur.

Trump's use of media went beyond traditional outlets. As the digital age took hold, he began to explore new forms of media to stay connected with his audience. By the mid-2000s, social media platforms like Twitter were beginning to change the way public figures interacted with the world. Trump was quick to recognize the potential of these platforms to amplify his message without the need for intermediaries like television networks or newspapers. This direct connection with the public would prove instrumental in the years to come, as Trump increasingly bypassed traditional media to speak directly to his supporters.

The expansion of the Trump brand wasn't limited to the United States. With *The Apprentice* giving him global exposure, Trump began to explore international opportunities. He partnered with developers around the world to bring Trump-branded buildings to major cities such as Istanbul, Manila, and Dubai. These ventures extended the reach of the Trump brand far beyond its American roots, positioning Trump as a global figure in luxury real estate. Each new Trump-branded tower or hotel became a symbol of success in its own right, carrying the same aura of prestige that had been cultivated through *The Apprentice*.

By leveraging his media power, Trump transformed himself from a New York real estate mogul into a global brand. He understood that *The Apprentice* had given him a new level of visibility and influence, and he used that platform to expand his empire in ways that were previously unimaginable. Every product, service, or venture that bore the Trump name was a reflection of the image he had crafted on television: successful, bold, and unapologetically luxurious. Trump's ability to blend media exposure with business strategy was nothing short of remarkable, and it laid the groundwork for the expansion of his brand into a vast array of industries. The Trump brand was no longer just about buildings; it had become a symbol of ambition and success, and it was all made possible by the power of media.

Trump's Strategic Control Over His Media Narrative

Donald Trump's ability to manage and control his media narrative played a pivotal role in elevating his personal brand during the years of *The Apprentice*. While the show provided a public platform for his business persona, it was Trump's strategic use of media outside the program that allowed him to maintain a constant presence in the public eye. His understanding of how to leverage the media for personal gain was key to shaping his image as a larger-than-life figure, and he took full advantage of the exposure.

From the start of *The Apprentice*, Trump's public persona was carefully curated to align with the image he had always aspired to present: a master of business, an unshakable dealmaker, and a symbol of success. He realized early on that in the age of reality television and 24-hour news, controlling how one is seen by the public could be just as important as the business deals themselves. In many ways, Trump's media strategy became a form of modern branding, where every interview, press conference, and public appearance was an opportunity to reinforce his identity as a high-powered, no-nonsense businessman who always came out on top.

One of Trump's key methods for managing his media presence was his savvy understanding of what journalists and television producers wanted. He knew how to generate headlines, often by making bold, controversial statements that would guarantee attention. Whether discussing business, politics, or pop culture, Trump had a knack for delivering memorable soundbites that would be picked up and replayed across multiple outlets. His frequent appearances on news shows, talk shows, and radio programs helped keep his name in the spotlight even when *The Apprentice* wasn't on the air. Trump's unfiltered, often brash style made him a magnet for media coverage, and he knew exactly how to use that to his advantage.

His business ventures, particularly the ones showcased on *The Apprentice*, were often intertwined with his media strategy. For example, when Trump opened a new hotel or launched a new project, he ensured that the press was there to cover it, turning even routine business announcements into major media events. The opening of Trump Tower Chicago, for instance, was covered extensively, not just as a real estate development, but as a symbol of Trump's expanding empire. Similarly, his golf courses and resorts were consistently framed in the media as destinations for the wealthy and powerful, further enhancing the prestige of the Trump brand.

Trump also used media opportunities to deflect criticism and protect his reputation during challenging times. Whether it was a downturn in one of his businesses, a legal dispute, or negative press about his personal life, Trump would often go on the offensive, using interviews or statements to shift the narrative in his favor. This strategy was particularly evident during his legal battles surrounding Trump University. Despite mounting lawsuits alleging that the program had defrauded students, Trump's public responses emphasized his success as a businessman and the value of the lessons taught at the institution. He positioned the controversy as an attack on his business acumen, framing himself as a victim of unfair scrutiny by his detractors.

Perhaps one of the most important aspects of Trump's media strategy was his ability to present himself as relatable to the average American, despite his vast wealth. While he flaunted his luxurious lifestyle—his private jets, his lavish homes, his penchant for gold-plated décor—Trump also made a concerted effort to speak in a way that resonated with everyday people. On *The Apprentice*, he often spoke about hard work, ambition, and the drive to succeed, themes that many viewers found inspiring. His blunt, straightforward manner of speaking, combined with his willingness to challenge established norms, made him seem authentic and relatable, even to those who would never experience the level of wealth he enjoyed.

Another key to Trump's media strategy was his keen understanding of controversy and how it could be used to his benefit. While most public figures shy away from controversy, Trump embraced it. Whether it was his ongoing feuds with celebrities, his controversial statements on political issues, or his frequent clashes with the press, Trump knew that being at the center of controversy kept him in the headlines. This tactic allowed him to dominate news cycles, ensuring that his name remained relevant and that people were constantly talking about him. Even negative press could be spun into a positive, as Trump understood that any publicity, whether good or bad, was valuable in keeping his brand at the forefront of public consciousness.

Social media also became an increasingly important part of Trump's media strategy as the platform grew in prominence during the mid-2000s. Trump was one of the earliest public figures to recognize the potential of platforms like Twitter to bypass traditional media and communicate directly with the public. While he wasn't as active on Twitter during the height of *The Apprentice* as he would later become, he used the platform to make statements, promote his ventures, and engage with fans. This direct line of communication gave Trump unprecedented control over his message, allowing him to speak unfiltered to his audience and respond to critics in real time.

Beyond just promoting his businesses, Trump used media to build a personal mythology around his identity. He presented himself not just as a successful businessman, but as a larger-than-life figure—a master of the universe who had achieved the American Dream and was now offering others the chance to learn from his wisdom. Whether through television appearances, magazine covers, or interviews, Trump's media presence was designed to convey the idea that he was not just rich, but a symbol of what anyone could achieve with the right combination of hard work, confidence, and vision.

In essence, Trump's control over his media narrative was a key part of his business strategy during the *Apprentice* years. By consistently shaping how he was portrayed in the media, Trump was able to create an image of himself that was as much a part of his empire as his real estate holdings. He understood that in the age of television and the internet, perception was reality—and through his savvy manipulation of the media, Donald Trump became one of the most recognizable and influential public figures in the world. This mastery of media would serve him well, not just in business, but in the political realm in the years to come.

The Global Impact of The Apprentice and Trump's Media Legacy

As *The Apprentice* continued to dominate television ratings in the United States, its success transcended national borders, becoming a global phenomenon that further solidified Donald Trump's status as an international icon. The show's format, which pitted contestants against one another in a series of business challenges under Trump's guidance, resonated with audiences worldwide. With international adaptations and syndications in countries as diverse as the United Kingdom, Brazil, and the Middle East, Trump's persona—and by extension, his brand—was now being beamed into millions of homes across the globe.

The global success of *The Apprentice* created a new level of visibility for Trump's brand that far exceeded the reach of his real estate ventures. His name, previously associated primarily with luxury skyscrapers in Manhattan, was now recognized on every continent. The core message of *The Apprentice*—that success could be achieved through hard work, competitiveness, and bold decision-making—was universally appealing. Viewers from London to Tokyo tuned in to see Trump's no-nonsense approach to business, his famous "You're fired" catchphrase, and his larger-than-life personality, which embodied the aspirational values of ambition and achievement.

This international exposure opened up significant opportunities for Trump to expand his business empire beyond American shores. With his brand now carrying global recognition, Trump began to enter new markets, particularly in the luxury real estate and hospitality sectors. Trump-branded properties began to spring up in cities like Istanbul, Vancouver, and Baku, Azerbaijan. These projects were often developed in partnership with local investors and developers who were eager to leverage the Trump name for its perceived prestige. The allure of staying in a Trump hotel or owning a residence in a Trump-branded skyscraper was not limited to American consumers; it had become a global symbol of wealth and status.

The branding strategy Trump employed was remarkably effective. By licensing his name to international projects, Trump was able to expand his empire without directly shouldering the financial risks involved in foreign development. This approach allowed him to maintain a presence in highly lucrative markets, while capitalizing on the global perception of the Trump brand as synonymous with luxury and success. In many cases, these international deals were structured in such a way that Trump's involvement was largely limited to lending his name and brand, while local partners handled the construction and operation of the properties. This licensing model further enhanced Trump's reputation as a savvy businessman who knew how to maximize returns on his brand.

The success of *The Apprentice* also helped to cultivate Trump's media image as a global business leader, a perception that further fueled his international ventures. His role as the authoritative figure on the show—delivering boardroom verdicts, dispensing advice, and guiding aspiring entrepreneurs—reinforced the idea that Trump was not just a successful real estate mogul, but a global business visionary. This media portrayal was integral to the success of his international projects, as it imbued them with the same prestige and allure that Trump himself embodied on screen. In countries where the Trump name might not have been as well-known before *The Apprentice*, the show helped introduce and elevate the brand to new heights.

Trump's global media reach extended beyond just real estate. The show's success allowed him to explore other branding opportunities in international markets. For example, Trump began to license his name to a variety of products in regions where his television presence had made him a household name. From luxury consumer goods to golf resorts, Trump-branded ventures began to appear in diverse markets, all capitalizing on the global recognition of his media persona. In each of these ventures, the formula was the same: the Trump name was used to convey a sense of exclusivity, success, and ambition, qualities that had been carefully cultivated through his media presence.

As *The Apprentice* grew into a global success, it also cemented Trump's place in the media landscape as a master of branding. He had built a business empire on the foundation of his name, and his ability to navigate the media world further solidified his influence. *The Apprentice* had made him a familiar face not just in the United States, but in countless countries around the world, giving him a level of recognition that few other business figures could claim. His media persona, crafted through years of television appearances, interviews, and strategic branding, had become inseparable from his business success.

Trump's media legacy, however, was not just about the deals and properties his name adorned—it was about the way he understood and manipulated the power of media itself. Long before the rise of social media influencers or reality television stars, Trump recognized that media could be more than just a tool for publicity; it could be a platform for building an empire. He understood that visibility and perception were just as important as the actual business transactions happening behind the scenes. By positioning himself as both a business mogul and a media figure, Trump blurred the lines between celebrity and entrepreneur, creating a model that would be emulated by countless others in the years to come.

In the end, the global impact of *The Apprentice* and Trump's media presence cannot be overstated. The show transformed him from a prominent real estate developer into a worldwide business brand. It gave him unprecedented access to new markets, enhanced his visibility on a global scale, and allowed him to expand his empire through strategic partnerships and licensing deals. More than that, it cemented his legacy as a master of media manipulation, a businessman who understood that the way he was perceived in the public eye was a crucial component of his success. Whether viewers loved or hated him, Trump's ability to dominate the media ensured that his brand—and his empire—would endure.

As Trump continued to leverage his media presence in the years following *The Apprentice*, the lessons he learned from the show would continue to influence his business and public life, ultimately shaping the trajectory of his future endeavors.

| 10 |

Chapter 10: Real Estate Masterpieces: Skyscrapers

The Trump Tower Legacy: Architectural Landmarks in Major Cities

Donald Trump's legacy as a real estate magnate is perhaps most closely associated with his groundbreaking work in the realm of luxury skyscrapers. The crown jewel of his portfolio, Trump Tower in Manhattan, not only cemented his place as a dominant figure in real estate but also marked the beginning of a new era in high-end urban development. Located on Fifth Avenue, one of the most prestigious and expensive streets in New York City, Trump Tower was conceived as a symbol of wealth, power, and luxury.

Trump Tower was not just another office building or residential space—it was a statement. Completed in 1983, the 58-story glass structure rose from the heart of Midtown Manhattan, commanding attention with its sleek, reflective façade. The building was designed by architect Der Scutt, and its bold appearance, with bronze-tinted windows and a cascade of terraces, made it instantly iconic. This was not a project built to blend in; it was created to stand out, much like Trump himself. The tower's interior, adorned with marble, gold finishes, and grand waterfalls, became a defining feature of Trump's luxury aesthetic, one that would later be replicated in many of his other projects.

Trump had a grand vision for the tower: it was to be a mix of retail, commercial, and residential space, with the top floors housing luxury condominiums that would attract the wealthiest buyers. The combination of these elements made Trump Tower a hybrid model in Manhattan's real estate market, offering both prestigious corporate offices and lavish residences in one soaring structure. The first few floors housed high-end retail stores and restaurants, including the renowned Trump Grill, which contributed to the building's allure as a destination for both New Yorkers and tourists alike.

At the time of its development, Trump Tower was a daring endeavor. Trump had purchased the prime piece of real estate from the Bonwit Teller department store, which had been a fixture in New York since the early 20th century. Demolishing the historic building to make way for his towering vision wasn't without controversy, but it also signaled Trump's willingness to make bold moves that others might shy away from. His decision to go vertical with such a high-profile, luxury development in the heart of Manhattan's busiest commercial district was a calculated risk. The project's success, however, proved that Trump had an innate understanding of what the market craved—opulence, exclusivity, and a prime location.

Trump Tower became a central symbol of Trump's brand. Its grand opening was attended by celebrities, politicians, and industry leaders, drawing widespread media attention. The buzz surrounding the building was not just due to its design or location, but also to Trump's ability to market the project as more than just a place to live or work—it was a lifestyle. He tapped into the desires of the city's elite, offering luxury apartments with panoramic views of Central Park and Midtown, custom interiors, and the ultimate cachet of living in a building that carried the Trump name.

The financial success of Trump Tower was staggering. The residential units sold at record prices, making Trump one of the largest individual owners of luxury real estate in Manhattan. The tower's commercial spaces were also in high demand, with prestigious companies eager to lease office space in what had become one of the most recognizable addresses in the city. Trump's ability to sell both lifestyle and location was a key factor in making the building a resounding success.

Following the triumph of Trump Tower in Manhattan, Trump sought to replicate his model in other major cities. His ambition knew no bounds, and over the next few decades, Trump-branded towers began to spring up in cities like Chicago and Las Vegas. Trump International Hotel and Tower Chicago, completed in 2009, stands as one of the tallest buildings in the United States and has become a defining feature of the Chicago skyline. Like its New York predecessor, it combined luxury residences, a hotel, and high-end retail spaces, reinforcing Trump's approach to real estate as more than just a business— it was a means of crafting an experience.

Similarly, Trump Tower Las Vegas became synonymous with luxury in a city already famed for its opulence. Completed in 2008, the gold-plated skyscraper added a new level of sophistication to the Las Vegas Strip. Unlike many of the city's hotels, Trump Tower Las Vegas is a non-gaming hotel, a decision that was in keeping with Trump's brand image. The focus was instead on luxury accommodations, fine dining, and exclusive services, attracting a clientele seeking the glitz and glamour of Las Vegas without the typical casino experience.

These towering structures, whether in Manhattan, Chicago, or Las Vegas, share a common theme: they are designed to dominate the skyline and the market. Trump's skyscrapers are not merely buildings; they are symbols of his vision, his audacity, and his belief in the power of branding. By attaching his name to these towering creations, Trump transformed himself from a real estate developer into a global brand, synonymous with luxury, success, and ambition. His skyscrapers were—and remain—monuments to his personal philosophy: always think big, aim high, and create something that no one can ignore.

The Trump Tower legacy endures as a testament to Trump's early success in real estate, defining both his career and the cities that host these iconic structures. His impact on the architecture and urban landscapes of these major cities is undeniable, forever intertwining his name with the world of luxury development.

The Acquisition and Development of Trump National Golf Courses

As Donald Trump's real estate empire expanded beyond sky-scrapers, he saw an opportunity to diversify into another lucrative sector: luxury golf courses. Trump's fascination with golf began long before he became a course owner. It was a sport that, for him, symbolized prestige, exclusivity, and the high-net-worth lifestyle that he aimed to embody in all aspects of his brand. More than just a personal passion, Trump saw golf courses as a way to further so-lidify his presence in the luxury market, and he approached this venture with the same ambition and meticulousness that had de-fined his real estate projects.

Trump's entry into the golf course industry came with the acquisition of his first major golf property, the Trump National Golf Club in Westchester County, New York, in 1996. At the time, the club was struggling financially, and Trump recognized an opportunity to turn the course into one of the most exclusive and well-manicured golf resorts in the country. Trump's initial investment in the club, which included significant upgrades to the clubhouse, landscaping, and overall facilities, quickly turned the property around. He rebranded it as Trump National Golf Club, infusing the property with the same luxury appeal that had worked so well for his skyscrapers. Within a few years, the Westchester club became a destination for high-profile members, celebrities, and business leaders, cementing Trump's reputation in the golf world.

What distinguished Trump from other developers entering the golf market was his attention to detail. He didn't just buy existing clubs and leave them to run themselves—he personally oversaw renovations, making decisions on everything from the layout of the greens to the design of the clubhouses. Trump wanted his courses to reflect the grandeur and opulence of his brand, and his personal involvement ensured that every property bearing the Trump name exuded luxury. From marble-clad locker rooms to gourmet restaurants, Trump's golf clubs became extensions of the "Trump lifestyle"—a concept that appealed to the wealthy elite who sought an exclusive environment both on and off the course.

Trump National Golf Club in Westchester was only the beginning. Trump quickly expanded his golf portfolio, acquiring and developing clubs in other prime locations. His vision was not limited to the United States; he aimed to create a global network of Trump-branded golf courses that would appeal to high-net-worth individuals worldwide. One of his next major acquisitions was Trump National Golf Club in Bedminster, New Jersey. This course, which was previously owned by an automobile magnate, was transformed under Trump's ownership into one of the most prestigious golf properties on the East Coast. Like Westchester, Bedminster attracted an elite membership base and became the site of numerous high-profile golf tournaments and events.

Perhaps one of the most iconic properties in Trump's golf port-folio is the Trump National Doral Miami, a sprawling golf resort that he purchased in 2012. Located in the heart of Miami, Do-ral had long been a popular destination for golf enthusiasts, but it was in decline when Trump acquired it. True to form, Trump im-mediately launched a massive renovation project, investing hun-dreds of millions of dollars to bring the resort back to its former glory—and beyond. Doral's most famous course, the Blue Mon-ster, was redesigned to be even more challenging and visually stunning. The resort's luxury accommodations, world-class spa, and high-end restaurants helped transform Doral into a premier golf destination for both professional tournaments and luxury-seeking vacationers.

Beyond his U.S.-based properties, Trump's golf course empire extended overseas with acquisitions like Trump Turnberry in Scotland and Trump International Golf Links in Ireland. Trump Turnberry, in particular, is one of the jewels in his golf portfolio. The historic course, which has hosted multiple British Open championships, was a personal passion project for Trump. After acquiring the property in 2014, Trump embarked on an extensive renovation, not only to the golf course itself but also to the luxury hotel and amenities surrounding it. Turnberry became a symbol of Trump's commitment to maintaining world-class standards in everything he touched. The property's picturesque setting along the Scottish coastline, coupled with its deep ties to golf history, made it one of the most prestigious courses in the world, further enhancing Trump's reputation as a major player in the global golf industry.

What set Trump apart in the world of golf wasn't just his abil-ity to buy and renovate properties; it was the way he branded his courses as aspirational destinations for the ultra-wealthy. Trump golf courses weren't just places to play a round of golf—they were luxury retreats where members could experience the finest in service, amenities, and exclusivity. His courses catered to those who wanted more than just a great game; they wanted an experience that aligned with their lifestyle of success and affluence. Trump's ability to marry the worlds of real estate, luxury, and sports into a cohesive brand helped him create a golf empire that was as much about business as it was about the game.

Another key element of Trump's success in the golf industry was his marketing genius. He leveraged his own celebrity status and media presence to elevate the prestige of his golf properties. The Trump name, already synonymous with luxury through his skyscrapers and hotels, became a selling point for his courses. When he appeared on television or in interviews discussing his love of golf, it wasn't just personal passion—it was also strategic promotion. Trump understood the power of his brand, and by associating it with the finest golf courses, he was able to attract a clientele that sought exclusivity and prestige in every aspect of their lives.

Trump's golf courses quickly became the site of numerous high-profile events, including professional tournaments, celebrity charity matches, and even political gatherings. The combination of world-class facilities and the Trump brand made his courses highly sought after for hosting prestigious events. These high-visibility occasions further cemented the public's association between Trump, luxury, and success, reinforcing the perception that to play golf at a Trump course was to experience the pinnacle of the sport.

In conclusion, Trump's foray into the golf industry was not just a business diversification—it was a masterclass in branding and luxury development. Through strategic acquisitions, meticulous renovations, and an unwavering commitment to creating world-class experiences, Trump built an empire of golf courses that not only expanded his business reach but also strengthened his personal brand. Each Trump National Golf Club became a living testament to the values Trump championed: excellence, exclusivity, and prestige. With properties that spanned the globe, from the United States to Scotland and Ireland, Trump's golf empire became a key component of his broader real estate legacy, further solidifying his status as one of the most recognizable business figures in the world.

The Development of Trump International Hotel and Tower

As Donald Trump expanded his empire beyond luxury real estate and golf courses, he sought to further solidify his global presence by entering the high-stakes world of luxury hotels. While he had long been associated with opulent skyscrapers and branded real estate, the idea of creating hotels that bore his name was a natural extension of his brand. Trump envisioned these properties as more than just places to stay—they were to be destinations in their own right, offering unparalleled luxury, world-class amenities, and the prestige that came with staying at a Trump-branded property. One of his most ambitious ventures in this domain was the development of the Trump International Hotel and Tower, a series of mixed-use skyscrapers that would define his approach to hospitality.

The flagship of this collection, the Trump International Hotel and Tower in New York City, set the tone for what would become a defining part of Trump's business legacy. Located in Columbus Circle, at the crossroads of Central Park and the city's bustling business district, this tower became a symbol of both luxury and convenience. Originally built as the Gulf & Western Building, Trump saw an opportunity in the aging structure, acquiring it in the mid-1990s and undertaking a massive renovation to transform it into a world-class hotel and residential tower. When the Trump

International Hotel and Tower opened in 1997, it quickly became one of the most prestigious addresses in the city, attracting a clientele that appreciated the combination of prime location, five-star amenities, and the Trump name.

The renovation was a hallmark of Trump's strategy: taking an underperforming property and turning it into a high-value asset. The newly revamped tower featured luxury condominiums on the upper floors and a hotel on the lower levels, offering residents and guests breathtaking views of Central Park and the Manhattan skyline. The hotel itself was designed to cater to the highest-end clientele, with suites that rivaled the finest accommodations in the world. From the moment guests walked into the marble-clad lobby, they were greeted with the kind of opulence that had become synonymous with Trump's brand. The service was designed to match the luxury of the surroundings, with personal concierges, world-class dining, and exclusive access to some of the finest amenities the city had to offer.

What set the Trump International Hotel and Tower apart from other luxury hotels in Manhattan was not only its prime location and opulent design but also its focus on long-term value. The residential units, which sold for record-breaking prices, attracted international buyers who wanted more than just a home in the city—they wanted the prestige of living in a building that carried the Trump name. The combination of residential and hotel space allowed Trump to maximize the financial potential of the tower, creating a model that would be replicated in other cities around the world.

Following the success of the New York property, Trump expanded the Trump International Hotel and Tower concept to other major global cities. Chicago became one of the first, with the Trump International Hotel and Tower Chicago opening its doors in 2009. This 98-story skyscraper, one of the tallest in the Western Hemisphere, embodied Trump's vision of luxury on an even grander scale. Like its New York counterpart, the Chicago tower featured a mix of hotel rooms and luxury condominiums, along with an array of amenities that included Michelin-starred dining, a full-service spa, and extensive event spaces. The building's sleek, modern design, with its reflective glass façade, made it a standout on the Chicago skyline, while the Trump brand ensured that it attracted some of the city's most influential residents and visitors.

The Chicago tower also became a symbol of Trump's ability to weather economic storms. The project was launched during the mid-2000s, a period of economic growth and high demand for luxury real estate, but it faced challenges as the 2008 financial crisis hit just before its completion. Many developers would have struggled to survive such a setback, but Trump's reputation and business acumen allowed him to navigate the downturn, securing financing and adjusting sales strategies to keep the project afloat. By the time the tower opened, it was already one of the most talked-about developments in Chicago, and its long-term success demonstrated Trump's resilience as a businessman.

Trump International Hotel and Tower properties were also developed in other key cities, including Las Vegas, Toronto, and Waikiki. Each of these properties carried the same hallmarks as the New York and Chicago towers: prime locations, luxury accommodations, and a mix of residential and hotel space. In Las Vegas, for example, Trump opted to create a non-gaming hotel—a rarity on the Las Vegas Strip—catering to a clientele that sought luxury and privacy over the traditional casino experience. The tower, which opened in 2008, quickly became a popular destination for business travelers and celebrities looking for an upscale alternative to the city's more boisterous resorts.

In Toronto, the Trump International Hotel and Tower opened in 2012 as one of the city's tallest and most luxurious buildings.

Like its predecessors, the Toronto tower was designed to attract both wealthy residents and high-end travelers, offering everything from luxury penthouses to five-star hotel suites. The building featured a spa, upscale dining, and an array of exclusive services that helped differentiate it from other luxury hotels in the city. Despite its initial success, the property would later face financial difficulties, highlighting the risks inherent in global real estate development. However, the Toronto tower remained a symbol of Trump's global ambitions and his ability to bring his brand to major international markets.

Waikiki, another prime location, saw the opening of the Trump International Hotel Waikiki in 2009. This project marked Trump's expansion into the luxury resort market, with a property that offered both hotel rooms and residential units. Situated just steps from the beach, the Waikiki tower became a popular destination for tourists and investors alike, drawn by the combination of Trump's name and the allure of Hawaii's tropical lifestyle. The success of the Waikiki project underscored Trump's ability to adapt his brand to different markets, tailoring his developments to suit the specific demands of each location.

Through his Trump International Hotel and Tower developments, Donald Trump established a global presence in the luxury hospitality sector. These properties, located in some of the world's most desirable cities, became synonymous with exclusivity, luxury, and the Trump brand. By combining high-end residential units with five-star hotel accommodations, Trump was able to maximize the profitability of each development while reinforcing his reputation as a leader in both real estate and hospitality. The towers were more than just buildings—they were landmarks that defined Trump's approach to business: always aim for the best, and never compromise on quality or ambition.

Trump International Hotel Washington, D.C.–The Jewel of Pennsylvania Avenue

In 2016, Donald Trump made one of his most ambitious moves in the luxury hotel sector: the transformation of the Old Post Office building in Washington, D.C., into the Trump International Hotel Washington, D.C. This project wasn't just another addition to Trump's global portfolio—it was a statement. Located on Pennsylvania Avenue, just steps away from the White House, the hotel became one of the most significant and prestigious properties in his empire. More than just a business venture, the development of this hotel symbolized Trump's ability to take on high-profile projects in politically and historically important locations, intertwining his business and public persona.

The Old Post Office building, constructed in 1899, had long been a significant landmark in the nation's capital. However, by the late 20th century, it had fallen into disrepair, its grandeur overshadowed by the modern developments surrounding it. The building was a relic of the past, with crumbling interiors and outdated infrastructure. But Donald Trump saw potential in the historic structure. In 2012, the U.S. government awarded him a 60-year lease to redevelop the building into a luxury hotel, believing that Trump's reputation for high-end renovations and real estate expertise could breathe new life into the iconic property.

From the outset, Trump approached the redevelopment of the Old Post Office building with his characteristic flair for grandeur. He envisioned a hotel that would rival the best in the world, offering visitors to Washington, D.C., an experience unlike any other. Trump's plan included not only restoring the building's historic features but also modernizing it with the luxury amenities that had become synonymous with his brand. This blend of history and modern opulence became a hallmark of the project, reflecting

Trump's ability to balance the old and new in a way that appealed to his affluent clientele.

The renovation process was no small feat. Trump's team faced numerous challenges, including strict preservation requirements and a complex construction plan. The building's status as a historical landmark meant that many of its original features had to be maintained, while at the same time, the interiors needed to be completely transformed to meet the standards of a five-star hotel. Trump embraced these challenges, working closely with preservationists to restore the original clock tower, marble columns, and ornate stonework that gave the building its iconic appearance. At the same time, he spared no expense in outfitting the interiors with luxurious materials, including imported Italian marble, crystal chandeliers, and rich gold accents, all designed to create an atmosphere of timeless elegance.

The Trump International Hotel Washington, D.C., officially opened in September 2016, just a few months before Trump would be elected President of the United States. The timing of the opening added a layer of intrigue to the project, as it became a focal point of attention during Trump's campaign. The hotel quickly became a gathering place for political figures, diplomats, and high-profile visitors to the nation's capital. With its prime location on Pennsylvania Avenue, the hotel offered unparalleled access to Washington's corridors of power, attracting guests who wanted to be at the center of political activity while enjoying the height of luxury.

The hotel's interior was designed to impress, with soaring ceilings, opulent décor, and spacious guest rooms that catered to the elite. The signature suites, including the Trump Townhouse—a 6,300-square-foot residence within the hotel—set new standards for luxury accommodations in Washington, D.C. The hotel's restaurant, BLT Prime, became a dining destination for power brokers and politicians, adding to the hotel's reputation as a hub of influence. Every detail of the property was crafted to reflect Trump's personal brand of opulence, from the gold-accented lobby to the high-end shops and spa services.

One of the most notable features of the Trump International Hotel Washington, D.C., was its emphasis on service. Trump understood that for his hotel to stand out in a competitive market, it needed to offer more than just a beautiful setting—it had to provide an exceptional guest experience. The staff was trained to meet the highest standards of service, catering to the needs of an elite clientele. Whether arranging private tours of the city's landmarks or providing personalized concierge services, the hotel's team was dedicated to ensuring that every guest felt like a VIP. This commitment to service became one of the hotel's defining features, helping it to attract repeat business from high-profile guests and visitors from around the world.

While the Trump International Hotel Washington, D.C., was undeniably a success from a business standpoint, it also became a lightning rod for controversy. As Trump transitioned from businessman to President, questions arose about potential conflicts of interest related to the hotel's proximity to political power. Critics argued that foreign governments and lobbyists might choose to stay at the hotel in an attempt to curry favor with the new administration, raising ethical concerns about the blending of Trump's business interests and his role as President. The hotel, however, continued to operate as a popular destination, with Trump's family overseeing its management to avoid any direct involvement from the President himself.

Despite the controversies, the Trump International Hotel Washington, D.C., remains a testament to Trump's ability to transform historic buildings into modern luxury icons. The project highlighted his skill in taking on high-profile, high-risk ventures and turning them into successful business enterprises. The Old Post Office building, once seen as an outdated relic, was revitalized under Trump's ownership, becoming one of the most talked-about hotels in the world. The property stood as a symbol of both Trump's business acumen and his flair for spectacle, cementing his legacy in the hospitality industry.

In the years following its opening, the Trump International Hotel Washington, D.C., earned accolades from industry insiders and guests alike. It was named one of the top luxury hotels in the city, praised for its blend of historic charm and modern amenities. The hotel became a fixture of the D.C. landscape, frequented by tourists, business travelers, and political figures who appreciated its central location and lavish offerings. For Trump, the success of the hotel was yet another example of his ability to build an empire that spanned industries and continents, reinforcing the Trump brand as one of the most recognized and respected in the world.

In conclusion, the Trump International Hotel Washington, D.C., was not just another hotel—it was a bold statement of Trump's vision and ambition. By transforming a neglected historic building into a world-class luxury destination, Trump demonstrated his skill in navigating complex projects and turning them into profitable ventures. The hotel's success further solidified Trump's reputation as a business leader who could not only dream big but also deliver results, even in the face of challenges and controversy. As a jewel of Pennsylvania Avenue, the Trump International Hotel remains a key part of Trump's business legacy, embodying the qualities that have defined his career: audacity, ambition, and an unrelenting pursuit of excellence.

The Global Reach of Trump Hotels—A Legacy of Luxury

As the Trump brand expanded its footprint in the hospitality industry, Donald Trump's ambition for his hotels extended beyond national borders. Having established himself as a major player in the U.S. market with properties like Trump Tower, the Trump International Hotel & Tower series, and his flagship Washington, D.C. hotel, Trump turned his attention to creating a worldwide portfolio of luxury hotels. This global expansion would further cement his position as a leading figure in high-end real estate and hospitality, allowing him to tap into the international demand for the Trump brand's hallmark of luxury, exclusivity, and impeccable service.

One of Trump's most notable international ventures was the Trump International Hotel & Tower Vancouver, which opened its doors in 2017. Positioned in the heart of Vancouver's bustling financial district, this 63-story twisting skyscraper became an iconic part of the city's skyline. The building was designed by the award-winning architect Arthur Erickson, and its striking visual design—curved like a sail—added a modern touch to Vancouver's urban landscape. Just like Trump's other luxury properties, the Vancouver hotel combined both residential condominiums and hotel rooms, catering to wealthy individuals looking for either a short-term stay or a long-term investment.

Trump's Vancouver property represented his ability to capitalize on key global markets, tapping into the city's growing international appeal. Vancouver, with its mix of natural beauty and cosmopolitan lifestyle, was an ideal location for a Trump hotel, attracting high-net-worth individuals from around the world, particularly from Asia. The hotel offered 147 luxury guest rooms and suites, each equipped with floor-to-ceiling windows showcasing the breathtaking views of the Pacific Ocean and the North

Shore Mountains. The opulence and attention to detail that de-fined Trump properties were on full display here: from the lavishly appointed rooms to the state-of-the-art spa and wellness facilities, every aspect was designed to cater to the affluent traveler.

Vancouver wasn't Trump's only foray into international mar-kets. Trump had long recognized the potential of the Middle East-ern luxury market, where there was a high demand for branded real estate and hospitality projects that reflected wealth and status. The Trump International Golf Club Dubai, which opened in 2017 in partnership with DAMAC Properties, showcased Trump's abil-ity to adapt his brand to different cultures while maintaining the distinct style that had become synonymous with his name. The 18-hole golf course, designed by the renowned golfer Gil Hanse, became a symbol of Trump's global reach. Situated in the heart of DAMAC Hills, a luxury development in Dubai, the golf club was paired with high-end residential villas and a clubhouse, offering a complete lifestyle experience to its residents and members.

The success of the Dubai venture was a testament to Trump's understanding of international luxury markets. While the Middle East had long been a hub for opulent real estate and hospitality, Trump's entry into the region marked a new level of prestige for the area. His projects in Dubai attracted not only local elites but also wealthy investors from around the world, who sought out the Trump name as a guarantee of quality and sophistication. The project reinforced Trump's philosophy that luxury was a global language—one that transcended borders and cultural differences.

Another key region in Trump's global hotel portfolio was Asia. With booming economies and a rapidly expanding class of wealthy consumers, cities like Manila and Mumbai became prime targets for Trump-branded developments. In 2016, the Trump Tower Manila opened, becoming one of the tallest skyscrapers in the Philippines. This project, much like Trump's others, combined luxury residential units with high-end amenities, creating an exclusive community for the city's elite. The building's design, inspired by Trump's penchant for modern elegance, featured sleek lines, glass facades, and grand interiors. For Manila's growing affluent class, owning a residence in Trump Tower was not just a status symbol but a lifestyle choice, representing the pinnacle of luxury living.

In Mumbai, Trump struck a similar chord with the development of the Trump Tower Mumbai, a joint venture with India's Lodha Group. As one of the wealthiest cities in India, Mumbai was an ideal location for a Trump-branded project. The tower's 75 stories housed some of the most luxurious residential apartments in the country, complete with panoramic views of the Arabian Sea. Once again, Trump's understanding of international markets paid off, as the tower appealed to India's rising class of ultra-wealthy individuals who desired the exclusivity and prestige that came with the Trump brand.

In addition to his ventures in Asia and the Middle East, Trump's hotels extended into other parts of the globe, including Europe and Latin America. Trump's hotel projects were not just about providing a place to stay; they were about creating an experience that embodied the luxury lifestyle. His attention to detail, from the architecture to the amenities, ensured that every property carried the same level of distinction, regardless of its location. Whether it was a skyscraper in Vancouver or a golf club in Dubai, the Trump brand promised an elevated experience that combined opulence, service, and exclusivity.

However, global expansion was not without its challenges. International markets often came with unique risks, including political instability, fluctuating economies, and cultural differences. In some cases, Trump-branded projects faced local opposition or financial difficulties. The Trump Tower project in Toronto, for example, struggled to maintain profitability and eventually faced foreclosure. Similarly, Trump faced challenges in the Argentine market, where plans for a luxury resort in Punta del Este were complicated by local regulations and economic conditions. Despite these setbacks, Trump's global ambitions remained undeterred, and his brand continued to command respect in the world of luxury real estate and hospitality.

The global expansion of Trump Hotels marked a new chapter in Donald Trump's business career. His ability to take his brand across borders and into new markets demonstrated his entrepreneurial vision and business acumen. By leveraging the power of the Trump name, he created a worldwide network of luxury properties that catered to the world's wealthiest individuals. More than just hotels, these properties were symbols of Trump's legacy—testaments to his belief in creating the best, no matter where in the world he set his sights.

As Donald Trump transitioned from businessman to President, his global hotel empire continued to operate under the leadership of his children, ensuring that the brand he had built would endure. Trump Hotels, with its presence in cities around the world, remained a key part of his business legacy, representing the culmination of decades of ambition, vision, and a relentless pursuit of excellence. Through his global hotel empire, Trump's influence in the world of luxury hospitality would continue to resonate, long after his departure from the business world, as a symbol of his ability to dream big and build even bigger.

| 11 |

Chapter 11: Navigating Financial Crises

Early Financial Challenges in the 1980s

By the late 1980s, Donald Trump had become a household name, known for his bold real estate ventures and his ability to capture the media's attention. Trump Tower was a glittering success, the Plaza Hotel had been added to his portfolio, and he had even ventured into the airline industry with Trump Shuttle. To the public, he was the ultimate embodiment of the American Dream—confident, successful, and seemingly unstoppable. However, behind the scenes, financial storm clouds were gathering. Trump's aggressive expansion strategy, while dazzling, was based on high levels of debt, and as the economic climate began to shift, the cracks in his empire became increasingly apparent.

Trump's strategy during the 1980s was built around leveraging. He used borrowed money to finance the acquisition of his properties, taking advantage of a booming real estate market and low interest rates. This approach allowed him to grow his portfolio quickly and buy some of the most iconic properties in New York. Trump's confidence in his ability to turn these high-profile acquisitions into profitable ventures was unwavering. However, as interest rates started to climb and the real estate market began to cool, the heavy debt burden Trump had accumulated became a liability.

One of the most significant purchases Trump made during this time was the Plaza Hotel. Located on Fifth Avenue, the Plaza was a symbol of New York City's elite, and owning it was a dream for Trump. In 1988, he acquired the hotel for a staggering $407.5 million, significantly overpaying by most experts' standards. While Trump famously declared that he hadn't bought it to make money, but because it was "the ultimate trophy," the financial reality was less glamorous. The Plaza needed extensive renovations, which only added to the already high purchase price, and the income from the hotel was insufficient to cover the mounting costs. The hotel became a financial drain on Trump's empire, even as it boosted his public image.

Trump's foray into the airline industry also added to his financial woes. In 1989, he purchased Eastern Air Shuttle, a regional airline service that operated hourly flights between New York, Boston, and Washington, D.C. Trump rebranded it as Trump Shuttle, hoping to bring his flair for luxury to the aviation world. He invested heavily in upgrading the fleet, installing gold-plated seatbelt buckles and refurbishing the planes to reflect the opulence associated with his brand. However, the airline industry was experiencing turbulence due to rising fuel costs and increasing competition. Trump Shuttle, burdened with high operating costs and facing stiff competition from established carriers, failed to turn a profit. Within a few years, Trump was forced to sell the struggling airline, marking a significant financial loss.

These aggressive expansions were funded largely through loans from banks that were eager to back Trump's ventures due to his high public profile and his perceived ability to turn projects into successes. Trump's charm and confidence in his own abilities made him a magnet for credit. He became a master at negotiating favorable loan terms, and his reputation allowed him to secure financing for increasingly ambitious projects. However, by the end of the 1980s, the economic landscape was shifting. Interest rates were rising, making it more expensive to service debt, and the real estate market was cooling, making it harder to generate the revenues needed to pay back loans.

Trump's financial troubles began to surface as the value of his properties stagnated or declined, while his debt obligations remained fixed. His high-profile acquisitions, which had been heralded as triumphs, were now seen as over-leveraged risks. The combination of rising debt payments and underperforming assets created a financial squeeze. Trump's business empire, once a shining example of success, was teetering on the edge of collapse.

In response to the growing financial pressure, Trump initially relied on his personal brand to maintain confidence among lenders and investors. His media presence remained strong, and he continued to present an image of success and confidence, even as the financial realities grew dire. He understood the power of perception in business, and for a time, his ability to project an image of success allowed him to keep the banks at bay. However, as the 1980s drew to a close, the financial challenges were becoming too large to ignore.

The late 1980s marked a turning point for Trump's empire. The very strategies that had fueled his rapid rise—leveraging debt, acquiring high-profile assets, and relying on his brand—had now created a precarious situation. Trump's business was facing a perfect storm: a cooling real estate market, rising debt obligations, and underperforming assets. This period would test Trump's resilience as an entrepreneur and set the stage for the financial crises of the early 1990s, where his ability to negotiate, restructure, and rebuild would be pushed to its limits.

Though Trump's early financial challenges were formidable, they also laid the groundwork for his later successes. They taught him valuable lessons about risk, debt, and the importance of liquidity. These lessons would prove critical as he navigated the financial crises of the 1990s and beyond, emerging with a renewed focus on branding, media, and more calculated business ventures. In many ways, these early financial struggles shaped Trump's approach to business for the rest of his career.

The 1990s Bankruptcy Restructurings

The financial storm that had been building in the late 1980s came crashing down on Donald Trump's empire in the early 1990s. By 1991, he found himself in a precarious position: his properties, including the Plaza Hotel, Trump Tower, and his Atlantic City casinos, were heavily leveraged, and the income they generated was no longer enough to service the vast amount of debt. The economic downturn, coupled with rising interest rates and a sluggish real estate market, had put Trump in an untenable position. The man who had been synonymous with wealth and success was now teetering on the brink of financial disaster. Yet, it was during this period that Trump displayed a remarkable ability to navigate the complex world of debt restructuring and bankruptcy negotiations, allowing him to avoid total collapse and retain control of his prized assets.

The most publicized of Trump's financial crises came in Atlantic City, where his three casinos—the Trump Plaza, the Trump Castle, and the recently completed Trump Taj Mahal—were hemorrhaging money. The Taj Mahal, in particular, symbolized both Trump's ambition and his financial overreach. Dubbed the "eighth wonder of the world," the Taj Mahal was the largest casino in the world at the time of its opening in 1990. Lavishly decorated and featuring the kind of opulence that had become synonymous with the Trump brand, the casino had been built at a staggering cost of nearly $1 billion. Trump had financed its construction through junk bonds, a risky move that relied on high-interest debt to complete the project. When the revenues from the casino failed to meet expectations, the high debt payments quickly became unsustainable.

By the middle of 1991, the Trump Taj Mahal was on the verge of defaulting on its debt, and Trump had no choice but to file for Chapter 11 bankruptcy protection for the property. This type of bankruptcy allowed Trump to restructure the casino's debt while continuing operations. It was a difficult moment for Trump—both financially and personally—as the bankruptcy filings became front-page news, and his carefully crafted image of success took a hit. However, Trump approached the situation with a characteristic combination of pragmatism and confidence, focusing on negotiating deals that would allow him to retain control of his casinos, even as creditors took significant losses.

Trump's strategy during the restructuring process was twofold: first, he used his personal charisma and negotiation skills to convince lenders that he was still the best person to manage the properties, despite the financial turmoil. Second, he employed a series of legal maneuvers to minimize his personal liability. One of the key components of Trump's restructuring deals was the ability to reduce the massive interest payments on the junk bonds that had financed the Taj Mahal. By convincing bondholders to accept less than they were owed, Trump was able to bring down the casino's operating costs and keep the business running.

The Plaza Hotel, another of Trump's high-profile acquisitions, also required a complex restructuring. Trump had purchased the hotel in 1988 for $407.5 million, financing the deal with loans that had high-interest rates. Like the Taj Mahal, the Plaza was an iconic property, but it was not generating the income needed to service its debt. Trump was once again forced to negotiate with his lenders to avoid losing control of the property. In the case of the Plaza, Trump agreed to give up some equity in the hotel in exchange for more favorable loan terms. This allowed him to retain a stake in the property, though it was a far cry from the triumphant acquisition he had envisioned just a few years earlier.

Trump's Atlantic City casinos and the Plaza Hotel were not the only properties facing financial difficulties. His airline, Trump Shuttle, and his yacht, the Trump Princess, were also draining resources. Trump was forced to sell off some of these non-core assets to generate cash flow and reduce his debt burden. While painful, these sales were necessary to prevent further financial deterioration. Trump Shuttle was sold to USAir, marking the end of Trump's short-lived venture into the airline industry, and the Trump Princess was sold to a Saudi prince. These sales, along with the restructuring of his real estate holdings, allowed Trump to focus on preserving his most important assets—his casinos, hotels, and commercial properties in New York City.

One of the defining characteristics of Trump's approach to these financial crises was his ability to shield his personal assets from creditors. While many of his businesses were saddled with debt, Trump had structured his holdings in such a way that much of the risk was borne by the companies themselves, rather than by him personally. This allowed Trump to emerge from the bankruptcy process with his personal wealth largely intact, even as his businesses underwent significant restructuring. It was a testament to Trump's legal acumen and his ability to play hardball in negotiations with banks and bondholders.

Perhaps the most remarkable aspect of Trump's financial troubles in the early 1990s was that, despite the public nature of his bankruptcies and the media scrutiny surrounding his failures, he managed to maintain a public persona of success and resilience. Trump continued to appear on television and in the press, emphasizing his determination to turn things around. He was candid about the challenges he faced, often framing them as temporary setbacks in a much larger narrative of success. This ability to control the narrative—both with the public and with his creditors—was a key part of Trump's strategy during this period.

In the end, Trump's ability to navigate the bankruptcy process and restructure his debt allowed him to survive one of the most challenging periods of his career. While he emerged from the early 1990s with a smaller empire and a tarnished reputation, he also came away with valuable lessons about risk, debt, and the importance of maintaining control over his brand. These experiences would shape Trump's business philosophy in the years to come, as he moved away from high-risk ventures and began to focus more on building his brand as a licensing empire. The financial crises of the 1990s tested Trump's mettle as a businessman, but they also set the stage for his eventual comeback, proving that even in the face of adversity, Trump was capable of bouncing back.

The Turnaround – Trump's Comeback Strategy

By the mid-1990s, Donald Trump's financial situation, though still fragile, began to stabilize. Having survived a string of high-profile bankruptcies, Trump shifted his focus toward a more calculated strategy aimed at rebuilding his empire and restoring his reputation. This period marked a crucial turning point in Trump's career, as he learned to leverage the power of his personal brand while becoming more disciplined in his business ventures. Instead of relying solely on massive acquisitions and debt-driven projects, Trump began to explore new opportunities that required less financial risk but had the potential for high returns. Central to his comeback was the idea of transforming his name into a brand synonymous with luxury and success.

One of the key components of Trump's comeback strategy was his decision to step back from owning physical assets outright and instead focus on licensing his name. The licensing model allowed Trump to extend his reach far beyond New York and Atlantic City without shouldering the heavy debt burdens that had plagued him in the late 1980s. Developers, hotel chains, and other companies sought to capitalize on Trump's name, associating their projects with the prestige and allure that his brand represented. Trump began licensing his name to developers for everything from skyscrapers to golf courses, collecting hefty fees without the associated financial risk of direct ownership. This shift in strategy not only revived his fortunes but also solidified the Trump brand on a global scale.

Trump's first major step in this new direction came with the launch of **Trump International Hotel and Tower** in New York City. Rather than taking on massive debt to finance the entire project, Trump partnered with Hong Kong-based investors to fund the construction, reducing his financial exposure. Trump's role was primarily as the face of the project, lending his name and expertise in exchange for a share of the profits and management control. The luxury condominium and hotel, located near Central Park, was a success and reinforced Trump's ability to market high-end real estate under his brand. The Trump International brand would later expand to locations in Chicago, Las Vegas, and even overseas, becoming one of the most visible parts of Trump's portfolio.

Golf courses became another key area of focus during Trump's comeback. By the mid-1990s, Trump had turned his attention to acquiring and developing golf resorts, a business that aligned well with his brand of opulence and exclusivity. His first major acquisition was **Trump National Golf Club** in Briarcliff Manor, New York, followed by the purchase of **Trump National Golf Club in Bedminster, New Jersey**. Trump applied the same philosophy to his golf courses as he did to his other properties: they had to be the best, and they had to bear his name. Trump's golf properties quickly gained a reputation for their luxury, world-class amenities, and, of course, the Trump brand.

While Trump's focus on branding and licensing was a major shift from his earlier strategy of direct ownership, he still pursued high-profile real estate projects, albeit with more calculated risk. In 1996, Trump took on one of his most ambitious redevelopment projects to date: **The West Side Yards**. This 77-acre site on Manhattan's Upper West Side had long been considered one of the largest and most valuable undeveloped tracts of land in New York City. Trump's initial plan for the site included a series of skyscrapers, a new convention center, and a television production studio. However, after facing years of legal battles, zoning issues, and community opposition, Trump ultimately scaled back his vision. In 1997, he sold the site to a consortium of Hong Kong developers for $1.8 billion, marking one of the largest real estate deals in New York City's history. Although Trump no longer controlled the development, the deal underscored his ability to negotiate high-stakes transactions and secure enormous profits, even if the final project deviated from his original vision.

As Trump continued to rebuild, he became more adept at using media and publicity to his advantage, ensuring that the narrative of his comeback was as much about perception as it was about financial reality. The media had always been an integral part of Trump's rise to prominence, and now it played a key role in his recovery. He actively courted journalists, hosted television interviews, and made frequent appearances in the press, always emphasizing his resilience and ability to bounce back from adversity.

Trump knew that maintaining his image as a winner—someone who could thrive even after setbacks—was crucial to both his business success and his personal brand.

Television played an even bigger role in Trump's resurgence when he ventured into the world of reality TV with **The Apprentice** in 2004. The show, which focused on young entrepreneurs competing for a position at Trump's company, catapulted him back into the limelight and reinforced his image as the quintessential businessman. Though the show's success would come later, the groundwork for Trump's media-savvy approach had been laid throughout the 1990s. He understood that in the public eye, perception often outweighed reality, and he masterfully crafted the narrative of his return to glory, even as his financial situation remained delicate in the early stages of his comeback.

During this time, Trump also made strategic moves to bolster his wealth by pursuing high-profile partnerships with investors and leveraging favorable market conditions. His relationship with the global elite—business tycoons, royalty, and heads of state—helped him secure deals and access to capital. Trump cultivated a network of influential contacts who could provide financial backing or open doors to lucrative opportunities. His larger-than-life personality, combined with a relentless drive to succeed, made him an attractive partner for those seeking to capitalize on his fame and expertise.

By the late 1990s, Donald Trump's financial picture was brighter than it had been in years. His real estate ventures were back on track, his licensing deals were expanding globally, and his public persona had been restored to its former glory. The Trump name, once synonymous with luxury and success, was now a powerful brand in its own right, detached from the financial troubles that had once threatened to destroy it. Trump's ability to pivot from debt-ridden mogul to branding powerhouse was a testament to his adaptability and tenacity. He had transformed his strategy, learned from past mistakes, and emerged with a business model that would define the next phase of his career.

Leveraging the Media – The Role of Public Perception in Trump's Recovery

As Donald Trump navigated the tumultuous waters of financial recovery, one of his greatest assets proved to be his innate understanding of the media and its influence on public perception. Trump had always been a media-savvy figure, but during his comeback in the 1990s, he took his mastery of publicity to new heights. He realized that while financial numbers mattered, controlling the narrative was just as crucial. If he could shape how people viewed him, he could leverage that perception to rebuild his empire. Trump's ability to harness the power of the press, television, and other media outlets became a cornerstone of his strategy, allowing him to reframe his failures as temporary setbacks and highlight his resilience.

One of Trump's key tactics was ensuring that his personal brand—centered around wealth, power, and success—remained unscathed despite his financial difficulties. Even in the midst of bankruptcy proceedings, Trump worked tirelessly to project an image of confidence and optimism. He regularly appeared on television talk shows, gave interviews to major newspapers, and hosted press conferences where he emphasized his plans for a comeback. Trump knew that if he could convince the public—and more importantly, potential investors and partners—that he was still the successful businessman they had always known, he could regain their trust and attract new opportunities. His approach was bold: rather than shy away from the spotlight, he leaned into it, making his struggles part of the larger story of his eventual return to prominence.

One of Trump's most effective strategies was his ability to blend entertainment with business. Long before reality TV became a dominant force in American culture, Trump had already recognized the value of creating a larger-than-life persona that people could connect with. His public appearances were often characterized by grandiosity and spectacle, whether it was giving tours of his opulent properties or boasting about his latest deals. Trump understood that people were drawn to success stories, and he crafted his own narrative accordingly. By positioning himself as a figure of immense wealth and influence, he kept the Trump brand alive even when his finances were in turmoil. The public saw him as a winner, and that perception alone opened doors for him, even when the facts behind the scenes were more complicated.

Trump also capitalized on his long-standing relationships with key figures in the media. Throughout his career, he had cultivated connections with influential journalists, editors, and television producers who were eager to cover his story. This network allowed Trump to maintain a near-constant presence in the press, ensuring that his name stayed relevant. He was not just a businessman; he was a celebrity, and that status gave him access to platforms that many of his peers did not have. Whether it was a feature article in *The New York Times*, a guest appearance on *Larry King Live*, or coverage on financial news networks like CNBC, Trump made sure that his narrative was front and center. Even during the darkest moments of his financial troubles, Trump was never out of the public eye, which helped keep his brand—and, by extension, his businesses—afloat.

Trump's adept use of the media also played a critical role in reshaping how the public viewed his financial struggles. Rather than allowing his bankruptcies to define him as a failure, Trump reframed the narrative by casting himself as a savvy businessman who was merely weathering the inevitable ups and downs of the market. He frequently reminded reporters and the public that many great entrepreneurs had faced similar challenges and that bankruptcy was often a strategic tool for restructuring debt, not a sign of defeat. This framing resonated with many Americans, especially those who admired Trump's larger-than-life persona and saw him as a symbol of American ambition. Trump presented himself not as someone who had been beaten by financial adversity, but as someone who was smart enough to use the system to his advantage, even in difficult times.

In addition to traditional media, Trump was also quick to recognize the growing power of television as a tool for reinforcing his brand. In 1997, Trump made his first serious foray into television production with the creation of *Miss Universe* and *Miss USA* pageants, events that further cemented his image as a purveyor of glamour and luxury. The pageants were broadcast to millions of viewers worldwide, giving Trump an even larger platform to showcase his brand. These events, while ostensibly focused on beauty, were yet another way for Trump to stay in the spotlight and associate his name with success and high-profile entertainment. His involvement in these pageants allowed him to continue building his empire through media exposure, connecting with audiences in ways that transcended the world of real estate.

But it wasn't just pageantry that Trump saw as a vehicle for his brand; he also began laying the groundwork for what would become his most successful media venture: *The Apprentice*. Although the show wouldn't premiere until 2004, Trump spent much of the late 1990s and early 2000s positioning himself as the consummate businessman, one who had not only survived financial crises but had come out stronger on the other side. He portrayed himself as

200 - BILL VINCENT

someone who could teach others how to succeed in business—an image that would later become central to *The Apprentice*. Trump's appearances on talk shows, in business magazines, and at public events all helped to create the mythos around his name: that of the ultimate dealmaker who could overcome any obstacle.

Ultimately, Trump's use of the media during his recovery was not just a tactic for surviving financial hardship—it was a deliberate, calculated strategy that allowed him to regain control of his narrative and rebuild his empire. By leveraging the press and television to continually promote his image of success, Trump was able to turn public perception into a valuable asset. The media exposure gave him credibility, attracted new partners, and allowed him to launch ventures with minimal financial risk. Trump's mastery of the media was a crucial element in his comeback, proving that in the world of business, perception can often be as important as reality.

By the time the 1990s drew to a close, Donald Trump had successfully repositioned himself in the eyes of the public and his peers. His financial troubles had not vanished entirely, but he had reestablished his name as one synonymous with luxury, resilience, and success. Through strategic media engagement, Trump had turned what could have been a career-ending chapter into the foundation of his next great act. His use of the press and television not only saved his brand but also set the stage for his future dominance in both business and entertainment.

Strategic Partnerships and Capitalizing on the Market Boom

While Donald Trump's ability to manipulate media and public perception was a crucial factor in his comeback, he also understood the importance of aligning himself with the right partners and leveraging favorable market conditions. As the financial markets rebounded in the mid-1990s, Trump seized the opportunity to reposition himself as a formidable figure in the business world, strategically forging alliances that would help him regain financial stability and propel him back to the top of the real estate industry. These partnerships, combined with a keen sense of timing, allowed Trump to capitalize on the economic boom of the late 1990s and early 2000s, creating new pathways for growth and expansion.

One of Trump's key moves during this period was to partner with powerful, well-capitalized investors who could help him fund major projects without shouldering all the financial risk himself. After the bruising financial crisis of the early 1990s, Trump became more cautious about taking on excessive debt. Instead of using his own money to finance new ventures, Trump increasingly looked to foreign investors, private equity firms, and wealthy individuals eager to associate their names with the Trump brand. These partnerships allowed Trump to expand his portfolio and return to high-profile real estate deals without repeating the mistakes of the past.

A prime example of this strategy was Trump's redevelopment of the iconic **40 Wall Street** building in Manhattan. In 1995, Trump acquired the historic skyscraper, originally built in the 1930s, for a fraction of its market value after it had fallen into disrepair. Trump's investment in 40 Wall Street turned out to be a masterstroke, as the downtown real estate market was on the verge of a resurgence. With the help of private investors, Trump undertook a massive renovation of the building, transforming it into a high-end office tower. The project was a commercial success and helped reestablish Trump as a key player in Manhattan's real estate scene. The deal demonstrated Trump's renewed focus on identifying undervalued assets and using strategic partnerships to minimize risk while maximizing returns.

Another crucial area of Trump's comeback involved his ventures into the global market. Recognizing the growing appeal of luxury real estate in international cities, Trump expanded his brand to other countries, pursuing projects in locations like Toronto, Vancouver, Istanbul, and the Middle East. In many cases, these projects were developed through licensing agreements, where Trump would lend his name and design input to a project in exchange for a percentage of the profits. This approach allowed Trump to benefit from the explosive growth of international real estate without the burden of owning or managing properties directly. His international ventures diversified his portfolio and helped him mitigate the risks associated with the volatile New York market, while also cementing the Trump brand as a global symbol of luxury and success.

Trump's partnership with major financial institutions also played a vital role in his recovery. In 1998, as the U.S. economy soared, Trump entered into a highly lucrative relationship with Deutsche Bank, which provided him with hundreds of millions of dollars in loans to fund new real estate developments. These loans were critical in enabling Trump to finance ambitious projects like the **Trump International Hotel and Tower** in Chicago and Las Vegas, as well as several other high-profile properties. By tapping into the capital offered by large banks, Trump was able to reenter the real estate market in a significant way, rebuilding his empire on a foundation of strategic borrowing and investment.

However, Trump's partnerships extended beyond just financial institutions and real estate developers. During this period, he also became involved in licensing agreements with consumer products companies, lending his name to a wide range of ventures, including clothing, accessories, home goods, and even bottled water.

The diversification of the Trump brand into new sectors allowed him to generate income from businesses that were far less risky than real estate, giving him an additional stream of revenue that further solidified his comeback. For Trump, the key was to exploit his personal brand as much as possible, leveraging his fame to secure deals that required little capital investment on his part but offered substantial returns.

This strategy was particularly evident in Trump's expansion into the world of golf, which became a significant part of his business portfolio in the late 1990s and early 2000s. As Trump rebuilt his real estate empire, he recognized the appeal of golf courses as both business ventures and brand showcases. His first major acquisition in this space was the **Trump National Golf Club** in Briarcliff Manor, New York, followed by the **Trump National Golf Club in Bedminster, New Jersey**, which he purchased in 2002. Trump applied the same principles to his golf courses as he did to his other ventures: they had to be luxurious, exclusive, and carry his name as a symbol of prestige. By investing in golf, Trump not only created a new revenue stream but also extended his brand into a realm where high-net-worth individuals could experience the Trump lifestyle firsthand. His golf courses became a reflection of his brand's ethos of excellence, luxury, and success.

Perhaps one of the most significant factors in Trump's resurgence was his ability to time the market. While many investors were cautious in the wake of the early 1990s recession, Trump saw the economic boom of the late 1990s as an opportunity to expand aggressively. He recognized that the real estate market was on the cusp of a new growth phase, fueled by low-interest rates and increased demand for luxury properties. Trump's ability to anticipate market trends and act decisively allowed him to capitalize on rising property values and a renewed interest in urban development. He understood that success in real estate often came down to timing, and this time, he was determined to get it right.

As the 1990s gave way to the new millennium, Trump had successfully navigated his way through one of the most challenging periods of his career. His ability to forge strategic partnerships, diversify his business ventures, and capitalize on favorable market conditions helped him rebuild his empire from the ground up. By the early 2000s, Trump's financial troubles were behind him, and he stood at the helm of a global business empire that extended far beyond real estate. His brand, once battered by bankruptcies and setbacks, had emerged stronger than ever, a testament to Trump's resilience, adaptability, and unrelenting drive to succeed.

In the end, Trump's comeback was not just about money; it was about restoring his image and proving to the world—and to himself—that he could rise from the ashes and build something even greater. The lessons he learned during this period would shape the next phase of his career, both in business and beyond, solidifying his place as one of the most recognizable and influential figures in the world of real estate and branding. Through calculated risk-taking, strategic partnerships, and a keen understanding of the market, Donald Trump had not only survived but thrived, turning what could have been his downfall into the foundation of his future success.

| 12 |

Chapter 12: Diversification and Investment Strateg

The Need for Diversification Post-1990s Real Estate Collapse

The early 1990s were a defining period for Donald Trump, not just as a businessman but also as an entrepreneur with the ability to evolve. The financial crisis that hit the real estate industry during that time had nearly taken him down with it, forcing him to reassess his entire approach to business. Trump had built his early empire on high-risk, high-reward ventures centered on luxury real estate, specifically in Manhattan. While his bold moves had worked well during the real estate boom of the 1980s, the crash exposed the vulnerabilities of a portfolio overly reliant on a single sector. The collapse of real estate values and his highly leveraged investments put him at the brink of financial ruin. By 1992, Trump was reportedly over $900 million in personal debt and his empire was on the edge of bankruptcy.

This near-disastrous experience was a turning point for Trump. The crisis had made it clear that he could no longer afford to stake his entire business future on real estate alone. Diversification became not just a strategy but a necessity. Trump began to understand that relying on a single industry—especially one as volatile as real estate—was too dangerous. It wasn't just about surviving the immediate crisis; it was about building a more resilient empire that could withstand market fluctuations. The lesson was simple: if one segment falters, others should be strong enough to keep the business stable.

Trump's diversification strategy didn't happen overnight, nor was it without its challenges. The first step was to stabilize his real estate holdings, which required difficult negotiations with banks and creditors. Trump restructured his debt, sold off assets, and focused on turning around key properties that had suffered during the downturn, such as the Plaza Hotel and the Trump Taj Mahal in Atlantic City. This period of financial triage allowed him to stop the bleeding, but it also made him realize that his future couldn't rely on real estate alone. He needed to expand into other sectors that would generate revenue without the extreme volatility he had experienced in the property market.

One of the key areas Trump began to explore was the world of licensing. By lending his name to various projects and products, Trump saw a way to monetize his brand without the need to invest large sums of capital or take on excessive risk. This move was a marked departure from his previous approach, which had centered on real estate deals requiring heavy financial commitments. Instead, Trump began to leverage his growing fame and the power of his brand to enter into agreements that would allow him to collect royalties and licensing fees, all without the need to own the underlying businesses.

At the same time, Trump's renewed focus on diversification extended into other industries. He began looking for opportunities in areas that aligned with his personal brand of luxury, success, and entertainment. This would eventually lead him into ventures as diverse as reality television, golf courses, and even beauty pageants. The goal was to spread his risk across multiple industries, ensuring that his financial success didn't hinge on the fate of any single sector.

This shift in strategy was about more than just managing risk—it was about positioning himself for future growth. Trump realized that a diversified portfolio would not only help him navigate economic downturns but also open up new opportunities in emerging markets. As the world became more interconnected in the late 1990s and early 2000s, Trump's willingness to branch out beyond real estate allowed him to capitalize on the growing demand for global luxury brands and entertainment. His ability to diversify into multiple industries, while still keeping real estate at the core of his business, became a key factor in his resurgence.

In hindsight, the real estate crash of the early 1990s was one of the best things that could have happened to Donald Trump. It forced him to confront the limitations of his initial business model and rethink how to build a sustainable empire. The crisis taught him that diversification was essential—not just for mitigating risk, but for creating a business that could thrive in any economic climate. This lesson would serve as the foundation for the next phase of his career, as Trump embarked on a new journey of expansion that would eventually make his brand synonymous with global luxury and success.

Expanding into Entertainment: Miss Universe and The Apprentice

Diversification for Donald Trump didn't just mean branching out into new industries; it meant stepping onto a stage where his charisma and larger-than-life persona could be monetized. This shift into entertainment wasn't merely a side hustle or a whim—it was a deliberate and strategic move that helped to rebuild his brand and financial standing after the setbacks of the 1990s. Trump saw that the entertainment world could provide not only new revenue streams but also something far more valuable: a platform for promoting the Trump name to millions, turning it into a global symbol of success and luxury. Nowhere was this strategy more apparent than in his acquisition of the Miss Universe Organization and the creation of *The Apprentice*.

In 1996, Trump made one of his first major moves into the entertainment industry by purchasing the Miss Universe Organization, which included the Miss USA and Miss Teen USA pageants. To many, this seemed like an odd pivot for a real estate mogul, but Trump understood the potential. The Miss Universe Organization had been struggling with declining viewership and relevance, but Trump saw an opportunity to not only revitalize the pageant but also use it as a vehicle to reach a broader audience. His goal was to position the Miss Universe and Miss USA competitions as glamorous, high-profile events that captured the public's imagination. By leveraging his business acumen and media savvy, Trump transformed the pageants into lavish productions that attracted top sponsors and major network deals.

Trump's approach was simple: make the pageants bigger, bolder, and more luxurious. He moved the events to high-profile locations such as Las Vegas and major international cities, and the shows began to feature top-tier entertainment and celebrity judges. Under Trump's ownership, the pageants became known for their grandiosity and drama, with Trump himself playing a central role in their promotion. He wasn't just the owner—he was a visible presence at the events, using them to project his image as a man of wealth, power, and taste. This helped cement his brand in a new domain, one that appealed to both American and international audiences.

More importantly, the Miss Universe Organization became a stepping stone for Trump to enter new business ventures and partnerships around the world. Hosting the pageants in different countries provided networking opportunities with global business leaders, politicians, and media figures, opening doors for future deals. As a result, the pageants were more than just entertainment; they were a strategic tool for brand expansion and global influence. Trump's involvement in Miss Universe allowed him to diversify into entertainment in a way that complemented his existing real estate and hospitality ventures, aligning his brand with aspirational ideals of beauty, luxury, and success.

But it was Trump's next move into television that would truly redefine his public persona and elevate the Trump name to new heights. In 2004, he teamed up with producer Mark Burnett to launch *The Apprentice*, a reality television show that became a cultural phenomenon. The premise was simple: a group of aspiring businesspeople competed in various challenges to win a job within Trump's organization, with Trump serving as the host and ultimate judge. The show's format showcased Trump's business acumen and leadership style, but more importantly, it was an hour-long infomercial for the Trump brand every week.

Trump's role as the authoritative, no-nonsense CEO—complete with his signature phrase, "You're fired!"—became iconic. Millions of viewers tuned in to watch, not just for the competition, but to see Trump himself. He was no longer just a businessman; he was a celebrity, a household name known not just for his wealth but for his persona as the ultimate judge of business talent. This portrayal on *The Apprentice* reinforced the image Trump had been cultivating for decades: a tough but fair leader who could make or break careers with a single decision.

The success of *The Apprentice* was staggering. It became one of the highest-rated reality shows of the early 2000s, running for 14 seasons and spawning multiple spin-offs, including *The Celebrity Apprentice*. Trump's visibility and influence soared, giving him a newfound platform to promote his various business ventures, from real estate properties to branded merchandise. It also generated significant revenue—reports suggest Trump earned millions per season as the show's star and producer. The show's popularity didn't just bring in direct income; it provided a springboard for expanding Trump's licensing empire, which grew to include a wide array of products such as ties, colognes, and steaks, all marketed under the Trump name.

What made *The Apprentice* truly transformational for Trump, however, was how it reshaped his public image. By positioning himself as the ultimate arbiter of business success, Trump blurred the lines between reality television and real life, creating a persona that was larger than life. The show gave him a platform to project his philosophy on business, leadership, and success to millions of viewers each week. This wasn't just about entertainment—it was a masterclass in brand building, and Trump was the star pupil.

Through his ventures into entertainment, Donald Trump effectively diversified his business empire in a way that expanded his influence far beyond the world of real estate. The Miss Universe Organization and *The Apprentice* were not just profitable ventures; they were powerful branding tools that helped Trump reposition himself as a global icon of wealth, power, and success. By leveraging the reach and appeal of the entertainment industry, Trump found a way to monetize his personality and brand on an unprecedented scale. This expansion into media laid the groundwork for the next phase of his career, solidifying his position as not just a real estate tycoon, but a global brand in his own right.

Trump's Licensing Strategy

As Donald Trump emerged from the financial struggles of the early 1990s, one of the most innovative moves in his post-crisis strategy was his embrace of licensing. Trump had built a brand around luxury, success, and high-stakes real estate, but after narrowly avoiding financial collapse, he realized that there were smarter, less risky ways to leverage the power of the Trump name. Licensing allowed him to monetize his brand without the financial exposure and risk associated with direct ownership or heavy capital investment. Instead of pouring millions into acquiring or developing new properties or businesses, Trump began to sell the rights to his name, allowing other companies to use it in exchange for licensing fees. This was a game-changer for Trump's business model.

At the heart of Trump's licensing strategy was the belief that his name itself had immense value. Over the years, he had successfully cultivated a public image as the ultimate businessman, the epitome of luxury and success. Whether or not people were familiar with the nuances of his actual real estate deals, they knew the name "Trump" and associated it with prestige, opulence, and business acumen. Trump understood that he could monetize this perception by allowing others to capitalize on it through a wide range of products and services that carried his name. The appeal was clear: if you bought something with the Trump brand, you were buying into the image of success that he represented.

The licensing deals spanned across a variety of industries. Clothing, accessories, fragrances, furniture, home decor, and even bottled water—all bore the Trump name at some point. For Trump, it was a masterstroke of business. By lending his name to these products, he wasn't assuming the financial risks involved in manufacturing, marketing, or distribution. Instead, he allowed established companies to handle those details while he collected licensing fees, royalties, or a percentage of profits. This strategy gave Trump a new revenue stream with minimal overhead or exposure to potential losses.

One of the most well-known examples of Trump's licensing strategy was his line of men's suits, ties, and dress shirts. Partnering with manufacturers and retailers, Trump's clothing line was marketed as affordable luxury—clothes that embodied the power and sophistication of a Trump-branded lifestyle, but at a price point accessible to the average consumer. The suits were sold in major department stores like Macy's, and while Trump himself wasn't a fashion designer, the appeal of his name carried enough weight to attract buyers. The brand messaging was clear: if you wanted to dress like a successful businessman, you wore a Trump suit.

Similarly, Trump extended his brand into home goods with products like mattresses, furniture, and lighting. These items were marketed to consumers who wanted to bring a touch of Trump-style luxury into their homes. The messaging behind these products was similar to that of his clothing line: by purchasing a Trump-branded product, consumers could align themselves with the aura of success and affluence that his name represented.

Trump also ventured into personal care with products like Trump-branded cologne and even bottled water. Trump Ice, his line of bottled water, was sold in luxury hotels and casinos, reinforcing the idea that every element of life, even something as simple as water, could be elevated by the Trump name. It wasn't just about the product itself—it was about the lifestyle it symbolized. Owning something with the Trump brand meant, in a sense, buying into the high-end, glamorous world that Trump represented.

This licensing strategy wasn't without its critics. Many questioned whether the products truly reflected the luxury that the

Trump name claimed to represent, and some even accused Trump of diluting his brand by lending his name to too many items. However, from a business perspective, the licensing deals were hugely profitable. Trump didn't need to worry about the operational complexities or risks associated with these businesses, yet he still benefited from the perception of his involvement. The companies using his name were willing to pay handsomely for the association with the Trump brand because they knew it had value in the marketplace.

One of the key reasons this strategy worked so well for Trump was his deep understanding of marketing and public perception. Trump knew that his personal brand was about more than just real estate—it was about the idea of winning, of being the best, and of living a life of luxury. He capitalized on that perception by allowing companies to use his name to sell their products, which in turn reinforced his image as a successful mogul. It became a self-perpetuating cycle: the more products bore the Trump name, the more visible and omnipresent his brand became. And as long as those products were seen as successful, Trump's own reputation as a business genius was bolstered.

Trump's licensing strategy allowed him to create a diversified portfolio without needing to own the underlying businesses. It enabled him to profit from industries far outside his original expertise in real estate, extending the reach of his brand into new sectors while minimizing his financial exposure. This approach not only provided Trump with significant revenue but also helped solidify his place in popular culture as a symbol of success. Whether consumers were buying a Trump-branded suit, mattress, or cologne, they were participating in a world that Trump had carefully crafted—a world where his name equaled luxury, and luxury equaled success.

Global Real Estate Ventures and Strategic Partnerships

While Donald Trump's name became synonymous with luxury products through his licensing strategy, his core business remained firmly rooted in real estate. However, after establishing himself in the U.S. market, Trump's ambitions took him beyond domestic borders. In the 2000s, he began to look internationally, eyeing major cities around the world where he could further elevate the Trump brand through high-profile real estate developments. These ventures were not only about expanding his empire; they were also about cementing his image as a global player, someone whose influence stretched far beyond American shores. This chapter of Trump's business career showcased his ability to form strategic partnerships and leverage the global appeal of his brand to tap into lucrative markets abroad.

One of Trump's first major international successes came with the development of Trump International Hotel and Tower in Toronto. Completed in 2012, this skyscraper exemplified Trump's vision of bringing New York-style luxury and design to one of Canada's largest cities. Like many of his ventures, Trump didn't fund the entire project himself. Instead, he partnered with local developers and investors who were eager to bring the Trump name to their city. This model allowed Trump to minimize financial risk while reaping the rewards of his brand's global prestige. The towering structure featured high-end residences, hotel rooms, and luxury amenities, all marketed under the Trump banner, ensuring that every aspect of the building was associated with his reputation for opulence.

The Toronto project was just the beginning of Trump's global expansion. Soon after, the Trump brand appeared in cities like Vancouver, Manila, and Istanbul, each time with similar success. In many of these ventures, Trump operated as the brand ambassador and licensor, rather than directly funding the developments. By partnering with local developers who understood the regional markets, Trump could focus on what he did best—selling his brand as the ultimate stamp of luxury. The strategy worked well: these buildings became status symbols for their cities, appealing to wealthy buyers and international business travelers who wanted to associate themselves with Trump's name.

Trump's ability to forge partnerships with powerful figures in these markets was a key factor in his global success. In Istanbul, for example, Trump formed a joint venture with Turkish billionaire Aydın Doğan, one of the country's most prominent businessmen, to develop the Trump Towers Istanbul. Opened in 2010, the twin-tower complex featured luxury residences and office spaces, as well as a shopping mall. The towers quickly became a landmark in Istanbul, not only because of their modern design but also because they were the first Trump-branded project in Europe. This partnership was emblematic of Trump's approach to international deals: he aligned himself with influential local partners who could navigate the regulatory and cultural complexities of foreign markets while he brought the prestige of his brand to the table.

In Manila, Trump's partnership with Century Properties, a major Philippine real estate developer, led to the creation of Trump Tower Manila, a residential skyscraper that became one of the tallest buildings in the city. Once again, Trump played a key role in marketing the project, lending his name and image to the development while leaving the local team to manage the construction and financing. The building's ultra-modern design and luxurious amenities attracted wealthy buyers from across Southeast Asia, positioning it as one of the premier addresses in the region. For Trump, this project was another example of how his brand could transcend borders and cultural differences, appealing to an elite clientele no matter where the development was located.

One of the most successful international expansions of the Trump brand came in Dubai, where Trump partnered with DAMAC Properties, a leading Middle Eastern luxury developer. Together, they created two Trump-branded golf courses as part of the larger AKOYA residential development. Trump International Golf Club Dubai, which opened in 2017, was a crowning achievement in Trump's global portfolio. The project not only featured a championship-level golf course designed by legendary golfer Gil Hanse, but it was also surrounded by luxury villas and apartments. The collaboration with DAMAC was particularly lucrative for Trump, as Dubai had become one of the world's most affluent cities, attracting wealthy investors and real estate buyers from across the globe.

The partnership with DAMAC also highlighted Trump's ability to navigate complex political and cultural landscapes. The Middle East, with its unique business environment and regulatory challenges, required careful consideration and a strong local ally. Hussain Sajwani, the billionaire founder of DAMAC, became Trump's key partner in the region, helping to ensure the success of their ventures. For Trump, this wasn't just about building a golf course or selling villas—it was about cementing his presence in one of the world's most competitive real estate markets. The success of the Dubai project further boosted Trump's reputation as a global real estate magnate, capable of thriving in markets far removed from his New York base.

Trump's global real estate ventures were not without controversy, particularly as his political career took off. Critics pointed out potential conflicts of interest, especially in countries where Trump's business partners had close ties to local governments. However, from a purely business perspective, these projects showcased Trump's ability to adapt his model to the demands of international markets. By forming strategic partnerships with local developers, Trump minimized his own financial risk while capitalizing on the prestige of his brand. This approach allowed him to expand rapidly into markets as diverse as the Philippines, Turkey, and the United Arab Emirates, proving that the Trump name had universal appeal.

Through these international real estate ventures, Donald Trump demonstrated his ability to diversify not only within industries but also across geographic boundaries. The Trump brand became a global symbol of luxury, wealth, and power, attracting buyers and investors from all corners of the world. Whether in North America, Europe, or the Middle East, Trump's real estate developments were not just buildings—they were representations of his unique business philosophy, one that combined strategic partnerships, risk minimization, and the powerful allure of his brand.

Licensing Real Estate: A Low-Risk, High-Reward Model

As Donald Trump expanded his real estate footprint globally, one of his most effective strategies was the licensing of his name to developments he neither owned nor financed. By the time the 2000s rolled around, Trump had perfected the art of branding his name onto high-end properties, allowing developers to associate their projects with the prestige of the Trump brand without Trump bearing the financial burdens of construction or development. This model, which separated ownership from branding, proved to be a low-risk, high-reward approach that contributed significantly to Trump's growing international empire.

Licensing real estate projects became an increasingly attractive option for Trump as it allowed him to capitalize on the enormous equity he had built into his name. The Trump brand had become synonymous with luxury, exclusivity, and success, and developers around the world were eager to leverage that reputation. By licensing his name, Trump would agree to lend his brand to a development in exchange for a fee, royalties, or a share of the profits. In return, the developer could market their property as a Trump-branded luxury building, attracting high-end buyers and investors who wanted to be associated with the name.

One of the key advantages of this strategy was that Trump was not putting his own capital at risk. In traditional real estate development, there are significant financial hurdles: securing financing, managing construction, navigating local regulations, and selling units. By simply licensing his name, Trump sidestepped many of these challenges. The developers bore the financial and operational risks, while Trump reaped the benefits of having his brand tied to a successful property. It was a model that allowed him to scale his business rapidly, moving into new markets without the limitations imposed by funding and capital requirements.

An example of this model's success is the Trump International Hotel & Tower in Vancouver. Opened in 2017, this luxury development was not owned by Trump but rather by a Canadian development firm, the Holborn Group. The 63-story tower featured residential condos, a luxury hotel, and high-end retail spaces, all branded with Trump's name. Trump's involvement in the project was limited to lending his brand and providing input on design and marketing, while the Holborn Group handled the financial and operational aspects. Despite not being a direct investor, Trump benefited from the project's association with his name, which helped drive sales of the condos and attracted high-net-worth individuals looking for a Trump-branded residence.

The same model applied to Trump-branded buildings across the globe. Trump Tower Punta del Este in Uruguay, Trump Tower Mumbai in India, and Trump World Tower in Seoul were all developments where Trump licensed his name to local developers.

Each of these projects was marketed as a symbol of luxury living, drawing on the prestige and allure of the Trump brand. In these deals, Trump's licensing fees were structured to give him a share of the profits or a flat fee, allowing him to benefit financially from the success of the project without needing to navigate the complexities of international real estate markets.

Trump's ability to successfully license his name to real estate projects around the world also reflected his deep understanding of global luxury markets. He recognized that in many places, particularly emerging economies, there was a strong demand for Western luxury brands. By partnering with developers in these regions, Trump was able to position his name in markets like India, South Korea, and Latin America, where affluent buyers sought out prestigious international brands as symbols of status. For many buyers, owning a unit in a Trump-branded building was a sign that they had made it into the elite class. Trump understood that his name carried a level of cachet in these markets, and he capitalized on it.

This strategy also proved particularly effective in markets where Trump's name held a certain aspirational quality. In countries like India and the Philippines, the Trump brand represented an American dream of success, wealth, and power. By associating their developments with the Trump name, local developers could charge a premium for units, knowing that buyers were not just purchasing real estate but an entry into a lifestyle associated with luxury and success. Trump's international licensing model created a win-win scenario for both him and the developers: the projects benefited from the brand's prestige, and Trump benefited financially without taking on the risk of ownership.

The success of this licensing strategy was evident in the number of Trump-branded properties that emerged globally during the 2000s and 2010s. By the mid-2010s, there were over 50 Trump-branded real estate developments worldwide, including luxury condos, hotels, and office towers. Each project reinforced the power of Trump's name as a global symbol of opulence, helping to further entrench his brand in the international real estate market. More importantly, the licensing strategy allowed Trump to expand his empire beyond the physical limits of capital and geography. He could be in multiple cities at once, profiting from his name in far-flung markets without ever stepping foot on the ground.

The model also highlighted Trump's business acumen in recognizing the value of intangible assets. While many real estate developers focused solely on physical assets—land, buildings, and infrastructure—Trump saw his name as a key asset in itself. He realized that the Trump brand had intrinsic value and could be monetized independently of traditional real estate deals. By turning his name into a marketable commodity, Trump effectively built an empire on branding as much as on bricks and mortar.

Licensing real estate developments also had the added benefit of diversifying Trump's portfolio. Because he was not directly involved in the financing or ownership of these projects, he was not tied to the success or failure of any one market. If one project struggled, his overall financial exposure was limited. Conversely, if a project thrived, Trump stood to benefit significantly through his licensing agreements. This approach allowed him to weather economic downturns or fluctuations in specific real estate markets while maintaining a steady stream of income from his branded properties.

In the end, Trump's licensing of real estate developments became one of the cornerstones of his global business strategy. It allowed him to expand his influence, capitalize on the demand for luxury branding, and profit from his name without the financial risks typically associated with large-scale real estate development. It was a strategy that not only helped rebuild his empire after his financial crises but also ensured that the Trump brand would become a global fixture in the world of high-end real estate.

| 13 |

Chapter 13: Trump Organization: A Family Affair

The Early Influence of Fred Trump

The Trump Organization's origins can be traced back to Donald Trump's father, Fred Trump, a real estate mogul in his own right who built a solid foundation upon which Donald would eventually expand. Fred Trump's career as a developer of low-income housing in Queens and Brooklyn provided the essential framework for what would later become the Trump family's sprawling real estate empire. Although Fred's projects lacked the glamour and luxury that would later define Donald's ventures, his approach to business was rooted in sound financial practices, hard work, and an ability to navigate the complex world of New York City real estate. These principles would profoundly influence his son's entrepreneurial path.

Fred Trump was a self-made businessman who started in construction at a young age, building his first house by the time he was 20. Over the decades, he would go on to construct thousands of homes and apartment buildings, particularly during the post-World War II housing boom. His company, Elizabeth Trump & Son (named after his mother), catered primarily to working-class families, building affordable housing units with government assistance. This model of utilizing public funds, particularly Federal Housing Administration (FHA) loans, allowed Fred to keep his developments profitable while also serving a social need. It was a strategy that required a meticulous understanding of government regulations and a keen sense of the market, both of which he passed down to his son.

Donald Trump grew up watching his father navigate these complexities with precision. From a young age, he was immersed in the world of construction sites, contracts, and negotiations. While Fred was not a flashy businessman—he preferred to operate quietly, focusing on practical, long-term investments—he gave Donald an early education in the fundamentals of real estate. Fred's philosophy was grounded in building solid, functional housing that met a need, rather than taking on risky or extravagant projects. He believed in controlling costs, maximizing revenue, and maintaining a keen eye on the bottom line, all lessons that Donald absorbed during his formative years.

Fred also instilled in Donald the importance of hands-on management. He was not one to leave the details to others, and his involvement in every aspect of his projects—from the acquisition of land to the laying of bricks—taught Donald the value of being deeply involved in his ventures. Fred Trump's developments may not have had the cachet of luxury Manhattan skyscrapers, but they were dependable and profitable, built with the care and oversight that ensured long-term success. Fred also had an uncanny ability to navigate the bureaucracy of New York's real estate market, securing zoning approvals and funding with precision. This skill was particularly crucial in a city where real estate was often as much about relationships and political maneuvering as it was about bricks and mortar.

Fred Trump's influence on Donald extended beyond business strategy; it shaped his worldview. Fred was known for his frugality and strong work ethic, traits that Donald would carry into his own business dealings. Even as Donald transitioned into more high-profile projects, the ethos of efficiency and cost-effectiveness that Fred preached remained a cornerstone of the Trump Organization's operations. Fred's ability to see opportunity in every corner of the real estate market—from low-income housing to government contracts—taught Donald to approach business with an opportunistic and adaptable mindset.

By the time Donald was ready to step into a leadership role in the family business, he had already learned the intricacies of real estate development from a master. Fred Trump's legacy provided Donald with the tools he needed to succeed, but it also set a high standard for achievement. As much as Fred was a mentor, he was also a model of success that Donald felt compelled to surpass. While Fred's empire was built on stability and consistency, Donald would take a far more audacious approach, seeking to elevate the Trump name to heights his father had never dreamed of.

In essence, Fred Trump laid the foundation upon which Donald would build his own empire. The lessons of hard work, attention to detail, and an understanding of the market's needs were ingrained in Donald from an early age, forming the bedrock of his later ventures. Though Donald Trump's ambitions would eventually transcend the modest housing developments of Queens and Brooklyn, his father's influence remained ever-present in his approach to business. The Trump Organization, in its early years, was a reflection of Fred Trump's legacy—grounded in real estate, driven by ambition, and built to last.

Donald Trump Takes Over and Rebrands

When Donald Trump officially joined the family business in the early 1970s, it quickly became clear that he had a much grander vision than the one his father had established. While Fred Trump had built a successful business through affordable housing developments in the outer boroughs of New York City, Donald set his sights on Manhattan—the heart of the city's real estate industry and a far more prestigious playground for ambitious developers. His takeover of the Trump Organization marked the beginning of a bold rebranding effort, one that would transform the company from a modest, family-run operation into a global powerhouse synonymous with luxury, wealth, and power.

Donald had always been drawn to the excitement and prestige of Manhattan. The glimmering skyscrapers, bustling business districts, and high-stakes real estate deals of the borough were a far cry from the more practical and understated projects his father had built. To Donald, success in real estate meant making a mark on the iconic skyline of Manhattan, and he believed that the Trump name could become a symbol of opulence and success. But he knew that to achieve this, he would need to break away from the traditional methods that had defined his father's business.

One of Donald's first moves in rebranding the Trump Organization was to shift its focus from low-income housing to upscale developments that catered to the wealthy. His strategy was simple: he wanted to associate the Trump name with luxury, and the best way to do that was by building lavish properties in the most desirable areas of Manhattan. His first major venture, the transformation of the Commodore Hotel into the Grand Hyatt, would serve as a blueprint for this new direction. The deal, which involved complex negotiations with the city, the hotel chain, and multiple financiers, showcased Donald's ability to think big and take calculated risks—qualities that would define his approach to business for decades to come.

The Commodore Hotel deal was not just about renovating a dilapidated property; it was about making a statement. Donald wanted to prove that he could succeed in the highly competitive Manhattan market, and he understood that the Trump name needed to be front and center. This was where the real rebranding of the Trump Organization began. Donald insisted that his name be prominently displayed on every project, a departure from the more subdued branding of his father's developments. The Grand Hyatt was a success, both financially and in terms of visibility, and it solidified Donald's reputation as a rising star in New York real estate. From that point forward, the Trump name would become synonymous with luxury, exclusivity, and high-profile developments.

With the success of the Grand Hyatt under his belt, Donald set his sights on even bigger projects. His most ambitious early development was Trump Tower, a gleaming 58-story skyscraper on Fifth Avenue that would become the crown jewel of the Trump real estate empire. Trump Tower was more than just another building; it was a symbol of the new Trump Organization. Featuring luxury condominiums, office space, and high-end retail, the tower was designed to cater to the ultra-wealthy and to further establish Trump as a player in the world of high-end real estate. Like the Grand Hyatt, Trump Tower was emblazoned with the Trump name, a branding decision that would be repeated on nearly every project that followed.

This shift in focus also extended to how Donald approached financing and deal-making. While his father had been cautious and conservative in his investments, Donald embraced leverage and partnerships in ways that allowed him to take on much larger, riskier projects. He became known for his ability to secure loans and navigate complex financial arrangements, using borrowed money to fund grandiose developments. This aggressive approach to financing helped propel the Trump Organization into new territory, expanding its portfolio and its reach far beyond the confines of Queens and Brooklyn.

Another key component of Donald's rebranding effort was his flair for publicity. He understood that building a successful real estate empire wasn't just about bricks and mortar—it was also about building a persona. Donald actively courted the media, becoming a fixture in New York's social scene and cultivating an image as the ultimate dealmaker. He became a master at using the press to his advantage, generating headlines and ensuring that the Trump name was always associated with bold, high-profile projects. This media strategy would become a cornerstone of Trump's business philosophy, helping to elevate his brand far beyond the real estate industry.

By the late 1980s, the rebranding of the Trump Organization was complete. What had once been a small, family-run real estate company had been transformed into a global brand, with Donald Trump at the helm as its charismatic leader. The Trump name was now synonymous with luxury, ambition, and success. This transformation would continue to shape the organization for years to come, as Donald expanded into new markets, new industries, and new ventures—all under the banner of the Trump brand.

In taking over and rebranding the Trump Organization, Donald Trump demonstrated not only his ability to think big but also his understanding of the power of image and perception. He had taken his father's legacy and redefined it, making the Trump name a symbol of ambition, wealth, and success. It was the beginning of a new era for the Trump Organization, one that would see it grow into an international powerhouse, with Donald Trump as its most visible and iconic figure.

The Deal-Making Mindset

As Donald Trump began to carve out his niche in Manhattan's competitive real estate market, one of the defining features of his approach was his relentless focus on deal-making. From a young age, he had absorbed the lessons of negotiation and financial strategy from his father, Fred, but Donald transformed these lessons into a personal philosophy that emphasized not just the importance of making deals, but mastering the art of negotiation itself. This "deal-making mindset" would become a hallmark of his business success and would ultimately shape the very identity of the Trump Organization.

Donald understood that every deal, whether big or small, was a chess match. It required a deep understanding of the other party's motivations, a keen awareness of market dynamics, and an ability to think several steps ahead. He prided himself on being an astute negotiator, often claiming that he could sense a weakness in his counterpart within minutes of a conversation. This intuition was rooted in a combination of experience, confidence, and the sharp instincts he honed over years of navigating the complexities of real estate transactions.

One of Donald's early and noteworthy achievements in deal-making was his negotiation of the Trump Tower project. The acquisition of the site, which was previously the home of a derelict department store, required a blend of creativity and strategic thinking. Donald was not just purchasing a piece of real estate; he was creating a vision for a luxury skyscraper that would change the Manhattan skyline. To make this vision a reality, he had to negotiate with various stakeholders, including local government officials, lenders, and the site's existing owners.

In approaching these negotiations, Donald employed a unique strategy. He would often start by outlining the benefits his project would bring to the community, emphasizing the economic growth and job creation that would result from his development. By framing his proposals as advantageous not just for himself, but for the greater good, he was able to win the support of key decision-makers. This tactic would serve him well throughout his career, allowing him to build essential relationships and gain the trust of people who would ultimately influence the success of his projects.

Another critical element of Donald's deal-making mindset was his willingness to take risks. Unlike his father, who favored a more conservative approach, Donald was unafraid to push boundaries. He understood that the biggest rewards often came from the biggest risks, and he embraced this philosophy wholeheartedly. In the case of Trump Tower, for example, he secured a series of loans that allowed him to finance the project, even though the market was uncertain at the time. His belief in the project's potential was unwavering, and his tenacity paid off when the building opened to great acclaim and financial success.

Furthermore, Donald's flair for showmanship played a significant role in his negotiations. He cultivated an image as a larger-than-life figure, a savvy businessman who could navigate complex deals with ease. This persona often worked in his favor, as many of his counterparts were drawn in by his charisma and confidence. He was a master at creating a sense of urgency, making it clear that his deals were exclusive opportunities not to be missed. This tactic not only helped him close negotiations but also enhanced the perceived value of the Trump brand itself.

One of the defining moments of Trump's deal-making prowess came with the acquisition of the Plaza Hotel in 1988. The hotel was an iconic landmark in New York City, and the opportunity to own it represented a significant coup for Donald. However, the negotiations were anything but straightforward. The deal required a delicate balance of persuasion, strategic partnerships, and a keen understanding of the financial landscape. Donald leveraged his connections in the banking industry to secure the necessary financing, all while marketing the Plaza as a prime investment opportunity to potential stakeholders.

In navigating the Plaza Hotel deal, Donald demonstrated his ability to remain composed under pressure, a quality that would become essential in his business dealings. He faced fierce competition from other interested parties, and the stakes were high. But through his relentless persistence and shrewd negotiating tactics, he successfully acquired the Plaza, further cementing his reputation as a formidable force in the real estate sector. The deal not only enhanced his portfolio but also significantly elevated the Trump brand, positioning it as synonymous with luxury and prestige.

Donald's deal-making mindset was also characterized by his ability to adapt and pivot when necessary. The real estate market is inherently volatile, and successful developers must be ready to adjust their strategies in response to changing conditions. Donald often found himself in situations where initial plans had to be altered due to market fluctuations or unforeseen obstacles. His capacity to remain flexible while still pursuing his overarching vision allowed him to navigate challenges that would have derailed less seasoned developers.

In conclusion, Donald Trump's deal-making mindset was a cornerstone of his business success. He blended strategic negotiation tactics, risk-taking, and a flair for showmanship to secure lucrative deals that would elevate the Trump Organization to new heights. As he transformed the company into a global brand, this mindset would prove instrumental in shaping not only his career but also the broader landscape of real estate development in New York City. Donald's ability to create opportunities where others

232 - BILL VINCENT

saw obstacles set him apart from his peers and laid the ground-work for the future successes of the Trump Organization.

Marketing and Public Relations: Building the Trump Persona

As Donald Trump solidified his position as a real estate mogul in New York City, he recognized that successful deal-making and project execution were only part of the equation; he needed to cultivate a public persona that resonated with both investors and the general public. Marketing and public relations became essential components of his strategy to build the Trump brand. Donald understood that in a crowded marketplace, perception was reality, and he was determined to control the narrative surrounding his ventures.

From the outset, Trump employed innovative marketing strategies that focused on creating a glamorous image for his projects. He was acutely aware that luxury real estate was as much about lifestyle and aspiration as it was about the physical properties themselves. To that end, he made it a priority to market his developments not just as buildings but as gateways to a lavish lifestyle. Each property was portrayed as an exclusive opportunity for affluent buyers to elevate their status. This marketing approach resonated with wealthy clientele who were eager to invest in the aspirational lifestyle that the Trump brand represented.

One of the most effective tools in Trump's marketing arsenal was the media. He cultivated relationships with reporters and editors, making himself readily available for interviews and press events. This accessibility allowed him to remain in the public eye and create a buzz around his projects. Donald mastered the art of self-promotion, often employing provocative statements that garnered headlines and kept the Trump name in the news. He understood that controversy could be a powerful marketing tool, and he was not afraid to leverage it. By positioning himself as a brash and bold figure, he appealed to a media landscape that thrived on sensationalism.

The launch of Trump Tower in 1983 marked a pivotal moment in Donald's marketing strategy. The project was not only a feat of architectural ambition but also a carefully orchestrated public relations event. Leading up to the tower's opening, Donald held extravagant launch parties that attracted high-profile celebrities, socialites, and influential media figures. The grand opening was a spectacle, complete with lavish decorations and an exclusive guest list, making it one of the most talked-about events of the year. The media coverage that ensued was overwhelmingly positive, establishing Trump Tower as a symbol of luxury and success and propelling the Trump brand into the national spotlight.

Furthermore, Donald recognized the power of branding in creating a lasting impression. He made a conscious decision to emblazon his name on all his developments, ensuring that "Trump" became synonymous with luxury and prestige. This strategy was particularly evident with the construction of Trump International Hotel and Tower in Chicago, where his name was prominently displayed on the skyline. By associating his name with high-profile projects, Donald transformed the "Trump" brand into a global symbol of wealth and success.

In addition to traditional marketing techniques, Donald embraced the burgeoning world of real estate and lifestyle branding. He developed a distinctive style that combined opulence with accessibility, often presenting himself as the quintessential businessman who understood the needs and desires of his affluent clients. This persona was further reinforced through his appearances in various media, including interviews, magazine features, and even television shows. His charisma and confidence translated well on screen, allowing him to reach a broader audience and solidify his image as a self-made millionaire.

A notable milestone in Donald's public relations strategy was the launch of his book, "The Art of the Deal," published in 1987. Co-authored with journalist Tony Schwartz, the book provided an inside look at his business philosophies and experiences, blending autobiography with practical advice on negotiation and deal-making. "The Art of the Deal" became a bestseller, further solidifying his brand and expanding his reach into popular culture. It not only showcased his success in the business world but also positioned him as a thought leader in the realm of entrepreneurship. The book's success allowed him to reach audiences beyond traditional real estate circles, making the Trump name recognizable across the country.

Additionally, Donald ventured into the world of reality television, which would become a significant part of his public persona. The reality show "The Apprentice," which premiered in 2004, showcased his personality and business acumen in a new light. The show featured aspiring entrepreneurs competing for a chance to work for Trump, and it provided a platform for him to display his unique management style and larger-than-life persona. "The Apprentice" not only enhanced his visibility but also reinforced the perception of Donald as a decisive leader and savvy businessman. The show's success led to numerous spin-offs and further cemented his place in popular culture.

Throughout this period, Donald Trump was not merely selling properties; he was selling a lifestyle—a glamorous existence marked by success, wealth, and influence. His ability to effectively market himself and his projects allowed him to differentiate the Trump brand in a crowded real estate market. By skillfully managing public relations and utilizing media opportunities, he transformed the Trump name into a cultural phenomenon that transcended the boundaries of real estate.

In conclusion, the interplay between marketing and public relations was vital to Donald Trump's rise as a global brand. He understood that in the world of luxury real estate, perception was everything. By leveraging media coverage, crafting a compelling persona, and associating his name with high-profile projects, he successfully positioned the Trump brand as an icon of success and aspiration. This focus on marketing would not only pave the way for future developments but also establish Donald as a household name, setting the stage for the expansive empire he would continue to build in the years to come.

Lessons Learned: The Blueprint for Success

As Donald Trump continued to navigate the turbulent waters of the real estate market in New York City, he garnered a wealth of experiences that would shape his business philosophy and future endeavors. The lessons learned during this period not only cemented his status as a formidable developer but also provided a blueprint for success that he would apply to his later ventures. In this final section of Chapter 3, we will explore the key takeaways from Trump's early years in real estate, highlighting the principles and strategies that would underpin his empire-building efforts.

One of the most significant lessons Donald learned was the importance of adaptability. The real estate landscape is inherently volatile, characterized by fluctuating markets and changing economic conditions. Throughout his career, he faced various challenges, from economic downturns to fierce competition. However, rather than viewing these obstacles as setbacks, Donald embraced them as opportunities for growth and innovation. He became adept at pivoting his strategies in response to market shifts, a skill that would serve him well in the years to come. This adaptability allowed him to remain resilient in the face of adversity, a trait that became a hallmark of the Trump brand.

Another critical lesson was the necessity of building strong relationships. Donald recognized early on that success in real estate often hinged on collaboration and negotiation. He invested time in cultivating relationships with key stakeholders, including lenders, contractors, city officials, and potential investors. By fostering trust and goodwill, he was able to navigate complex transactions and secure financing for his projects. This emphasis on networking laid the foundation for the partnerships that would prove invaluable as he expanded his portfolio. Donald understood that in business, relationships could be just as important as contracts, and he made it a priority to nurture these connections.

Moreover, Donald learned the value of branding and positioning. His experiences during this period underscored the importance of creating a distinctive identity for both himself and his projects. He understood that in a crowded market, a strong brand could set him apart from competitors. By carefully crafting the Trump persona—one that exuded confidence, success, and luxury—he was able to create a lasting impression in the minds of consumers and investors alike. This commitment to branding would become a cornerstone of his strategy as he ventured into new markets and industries.

The significance of strategic risk-taking was another key takeaway from Donald's early experiences. He often found himself in high-stakes situations where calculated risks could lead to significant rewards. In the case of Trump Tower, for example, he took a gamble on a project that many viewed as too ambitious. However, his unwavering belief in the potential of the building and his willingness to invest in it paid off handsomely. This lesson reinforced his conviction that fortune favors the bold, and it inspired him to pursue ambitious projects throughout his career.

Additionally, Donald learned the power of vision. He had an uncanny ability to see potential where others saw obstacles. This visionary mindset allowed him to conceptualize ambitious projects and translate them into reality. Whether it was envisioning a luxury skyscraper in a bustling city or dreaming of a brand that would become synonymous with success, Donald's capacity to dream big fueled his drive to innovate and excel. His early ventures taught him that having a clear vision was essential for overcoming challenges and motivating others to join in his pursuits.

Finally, the importance of resilience became evident during his journey. The road to success was not without its setbacks, and Donald faced numerous challenges that tested his determination. From financial struggles to public scrutiny, he encountered obstacles that could have derailed lesser entrepreneurs. However, his tenacity and refusal to give up enabled him to rise above adversity and emerge stronger. This resilience became a defining characteristic of the Trump brand, inspiring others to believe in the possibility of achieving greatness despite the odds.

In conclusion, the early years of Donald Trump's career in real estate provided invaluable lessons that would shape his approach to business for decades to come. His emphasis on adaptability, relationship-building, branding, strategic risk-taking, visionary thinking, and resilience laid the groundwork for the empire he would go on to build. As he transitioned from a fledgling developer in Manhattan to a global business icon, these principles would continue to guide his decisions and define his legacy. The blueprint for success that emerged during this formative period was not just a reflection of Donald's ambitions; it was a testament to the enduring power of entrepreneurial spirit in the face of challenges.

| 14 |

Chapter 14: Trump's Return to Business After Polit

Reassessing the Landscape

After serving as the 45th president of the United States, Donald Trump re-entered the world of business with a new perspective, but the landscape he returned to was dramatically different from the one he had left. The challenges posed by the COVID-19 pandemic, the ever-shifting real estate market, and the polarized political climate required him to reassess his approach and strategies. For Trump, it wasn't just about returning to business as usual—it was about recalibrating and seizing new opportunities while navigating unprecedented challenges.

When Trump stepped away from the presidency, the real estate and hospitality sectors, both integral to his business empire, had been shaken by the pandemic. Hotels were seeing record-low occupancy rates, office spaces were becoming less relevant due to the rise of remote work, and tourism was struggling to recover from global lockdowns. Trump's properties, including his iconic hotels, golf courses, and resorts, faced declining revenues. The landscape demanded a strategic pivot, and Trump, known for his ability to adapt, set out to understand the intricacies of this new market.

At the same time, the political climate had shifted, and Trump himself was at the center of it. His presidency had sparked admiration among millions but also strong opposition, making his return to business a double-edged sword. On one hand, his core supporters were eager to continue engaging with the Trump brand, whether through his luxury properties or branded merchandise. On the other hand, many critics were vocal about boycotting anything associated with Trump, putting additional pressure on his businesses to perform in a divided marketplace.

Despite these challenges, Trump saw opportunities where others might have seen insurmountable obstacles. His first step was to reassess his assets and determine which areas of his business could thrive in the post-pandemic world. In a landscape where office spaces were shrinking, Trump began exploring ways to repurpose his commercial properties for mixed-use development, combining residential, retail, and office spaces to appeal to new market demands. For his hotels and resorts, Trump began to shift his focus toward high-end, luxury travelers who were eager to resume leisure travel once restrictions lifted. He also considered expanding his brand internationally, particularly in countries where the Trump name still carried prestige and where politics played less of a factor.

The digital transformation that accelerated during the pandemic also presented new opportunities for Trump. E-commerce and online business ventures had exploded, and Trump's team began exploring ways to integrate more digital platforms into their operations. Whether through virtual tours of luxury real estate or expanding the online reach of Trump-branded products, the goal was to capitalize on the growing digital economy. Trump, always the master of media, also considered ways to further leverage his presence on social media and alternative platforms to reach his base directly, without relying on traditional channels that were often critical of him.

In this new landscape, public perception of Trump as a businessman had also evolved. For his supporters, Trump's post-presidency business ventures were a continuation of his defiant, outsider persona—a man determined to succeed against the odds. For his detractors, however, the Trump brand remained polarizing, and many were vocal about their disapproval. Yet, Trump had always thrived on controversy and attention, and he was determined to use this to his advantage, knowing that any publicity could keep his name in the headlines and his brand relevant.

As he reassessed the new business landscape, Trump's approach was to adapt, innovate, and rebrand while staying true to the core principles that had defined his empire for decades. Despite the many challenges, Trump remained confident in his ability to once again rise to the top, even in a market that was far more complex and uncertain than the one he had navigated before his presidency.

Rebranding and Marketing Strategies

As Donald Trump re-entered the business world, he quickly realized that rebranding was essential. The political turbulence of his presidency had left an indelible mark on public perception, and while he still had a loyal base of supporters, he needed to reposition his brand to broaden its appeal and navigate the increasingly divided marketplace. Trump, a master of branding from the beginning of his career, knew that a successful return to business would depend on reinvigorating the Trump name while retaining the qualities that had made it globally recognizable: luxury, power, and success.

Trump's rebranding effort began by aligning his business ventures with a fresh narrative—one that highlighted his resilience and achievements, not just as a businessman, but as a former president who had weathered the storms of political controversy. His marketing team crafted campaigns that showcased his status as a symbol of American success, tapping into the notion that his life story was one of fighting adversity and overcoming obstacles. This theme of perseverance became central to how the Trump brand was repositioned. The message was clear: Donald Trump was not just a businessman but a figure who had stood up to the political establishment and was now channeling that same determination back into his businesses.

In rebranding, Trump was careful to emphasize the continuity of his brand's core values—luxury, exclusivity, and boldness—while subtly modernizing the image to resonate with a new generation of consumers. His high-end properties, golf courses, and resorts continued to market themselves as symbols of opulence, but with an added focus on experiential luxury. This shift was particularly evident in Trump's hospitality division, where the new marketing strategies highlighted experiences that aligned with the post-pandemic desire for personalized, luxurious escapes. Trump hotels, for example, leaned into creating exclusive, bespoke travel experiences tailored for high-net-worth individuals seeking privacy and comfort in the wake of COVID-19's impact on global travel.

Moreover, the Trump Organization began to explore opportunities in emerging sectors that allowed for innovative brand extensions. Realizing the potential in the burgeoning wellness and sustainable luxury markets, Trump began investing in eco-friendly projects, such as sustainable resorts and energy-efficient luxury real estate. This strategic pivot not only aimed to attract the attention of affluent, socially-conscious consumers but also worked to position the Trump brand as one that was evolving with global trends, not just clinging to past glory. By adapting to new market demands, Trump sought to demonstrate that his brand could thrive in the modern business environment, while still staying true to its roots in elegance and grandeur.

At the core of this rebranding was a deliberate effort to focus on his achievements and status as a successful businessman before and after his presidency. Marketing campaigns heavily featured images of Trump in powerful, executive settings—towering over blueprints, inspecting properties, or hosting elite events at his resorts—reasserting the image of Trump as a man in control. His businesses, particularly his hotels and golf courses, began hosting events and conferences that attracted global leaders and influencers, further positioning his properties as centers of power and influence. These efforts aimed to reinforce the idea that, regardless of his time in politics, Trump was still a major player on the world stage.

Another key component of Trump's rebranding strategy was to leverage his immense following on social media. Trump had always been a savvy user of media to promote his businesses, and even after his departure from mainstream platforms, he continued to engage with his supporters through alternative media and digital channels. This direct engagement not only kept his brand relevant but also allowed him to bypass traditional media outlets that were often critical of him. By using these platforms to promote his businesses, Trump was able to tap into his loyal base, reminding them that the Trump brand was still synonymous with success.

His team also focused on re-establishing relationships with partners and collaborators in industries that aligned with his vision. Trump knew that brand strength was not just about public perception but about strategic alliances. The Trump Organization sought to form new partnerships in real estate, entertainment, and even technology, aiming to bolster the brand's relevance in a fast-evolving world. These partnerships were designed to open doors to new markets and opportunities, ensuring that the Trump name remained at the forefront of luxury and innovation.

Through these rebranding and marketing efforts, Trump managed to refocus the narrative surrounding his brand. While the political associations with his name could never be completely erased, his strategy was to remind the world that the Trump empire was built long before politics and would continue to flourish after. By reinforcing the message of strength, resilience, and luxury, Trump's rebranding was a powerful testament to his ability to adapt and thrive in the face of adversity. The Trump brand, as reimagined after his presidency, stood poised to take on the future, once again proving that Donald Trump was not just a businessman but a brand in and of himself.

Revitalizing Real Estate Holdings

As Donald Trump re-immersed himself in the business world, one of his primary focuses was revitalizing his real estate holdings. The Trump Organization had always been synonymous with luxury properties, from skyscrapers to golf courses and resorts. However, the market Trump returned to in the wake of the pandemic was deeply affected, and he had to rethink how to adapt his properties to meet new demands. Real estate, always central to his empire, became a cornerstone of his post-political comeback strategy.

Trump's initial step was to assess the performance of his key properties. Many of his signature assets, such as Trump Tower in New York and the Trump International Hotels, were struggling with reduced occupancy rates and fluctuating real estate values. The pandemic had led to a reduction in demand for both commercial and residential space, particularly in urban centers where Trump had made some of his most notable investments. However,

Trump had always thrived in a volatile market, and this downturn was no different.

One of his early moves was to focus on repurposing some of his iconic properties to fit the changing needs of the market. As remote work gained popularity, demand for traditional office spaces dropped. Trump's approach to this shift was twofold: he saw an opportunity to convert underutilized office spaces into mixed-use developments, combining high-end residential, retail, and office areas in key urban locations. For example, in Manhattan, Trump explored plans to redevelop some of his commercial real estate holdings into luxury residential units, catering to a growing class of affluent buyers seeking larger living spaces as remote work became the norm.

At the same time, Trump sought to capitalize on the resurgence in suburban and vacation home markets. The pandemic had sparked a migration of high-net-worth individuals away from dense urban areas and into more spacious, luxurious suburban environments, particularly in vacation destinations. Trump's sprawling golf courses and resorts, which were previously focused on tourism and leisure, became prime candidates for development into residential communities. By converting sections of these properties into exclusive, gated communities, Trump tapped into a trend where wealthy buyers sought expansive, secluded homes in scenic locales. His golf courses in Florida, New Jersey, and Scotland were among those poised for this transformation, as they already attracted a high-end clientele and had the potential to offer both leisure and luxury living.

In addition to these redevelopment plans, Trump began exploring international real estate markets with renewed interest. His brand still carried significant weight in regions like the Middle East, South America, and parts of Asia, where luxury development was booming, and where his political past was less polarizing.

Trump's team pursued new hotel and residential developments in countries eager to attract foreign investment and capitalize on the prestige of the Trump name. This international expansion was a crucial part of his strategy to diversify his holdings and reduce the reliance on U.S.-based real estate, which was more vulnerable to political and economic fluctuations.

Another critical component of Trump's real estate revitalization was sustainability. While Trump had previously avoided deep engagement with the green building movement, post-pandemic market shifts and the increasing importance of eco-friendly development offered new opportunities. Trump recognized that sustainability was no longer a niche market but a mainstream demand, particularly among younger, wealthy buyers. To align his brand with this growing trend, Trump's organization began incorporating energy-efficient designs and environmentally friendly technologies into new projects. From solar energy installations at his golf courses to green-certified residential developments, Trump sought to modernize his portfolio in a way that attracted forward-thinking buyers without compromising the luxury image he had built over decades.

Trump also capitalized on his reputation for hosting high-profile events at his properties to draw attention to his revitalized holdings. His resorts and hotels began hosting international summits, golf tournaments, and exclusive gatherings, ensuring that the Trump brand remained synonymous with power and luxury. These events not only generated revenue but also provided high-visibility platforms for Trump's reimagined real estate ventures. By showcasing his properties to global leaders, celebrities, and influential figures, Trump reaffirmed the prestige and relevance of his real estate empire.

Despite the challenges posed by the shifting market and the shadow of his political career, Trump's revitalization of his real estate holdings demonstrated his ability to adapt and innovate. His willingness to embrace new trends, such as sustainability and mixed-use developments, coupled with his continued focus on high-end luxury, allowed Trump to position his properties for future growth. As always, Trump's strategy revolved around understanding the desires of the elite and creating spaces that reflected his larger-than-life persona—grand, bold, and undeniably Trump. Through this approach, he aimed to ensure that his real estate holdings would not just survive but thrive in the post-pandemic world.

Expanding the Hospitality Empire

Donald Trump's hospitality empire, anchored by his high-end hotels and resorts, had long been a symbol of luxury and exclusivity. However, after returning to the business world post-presidency, he faced a dramatically changed hospitality industry. The global pandemic had left a significant impact on tourism and travel, forcing many companies to reassess their strategies. Trump, always quick to seize an opportunity, began refocusing his hospitality empire to adapt to the new market realities and consumer preferences while maintaining the opulent image that had made his brand famous.

One of Trump's key strategies was to double down on domestic travel markets, particularly in the United States. With international travel heavily restricted during the pandemic, many high-end travelers turned to luxury resorts within their home countries. Trump's properties, such as Mar-a-Lago in Florida and Trump National Doral in Miami, were perfectly positioned to capitalize on this trend. These properties, known for their expansive grounds and exclusive amenities, became ideal destinations for wealthy travelers seeking both safety and luxury in their getaways. By offering high levels of privacy, customized services, and adherence to stringent health protocols, Trump's resorts quickly adapted to meet the demand for safe, luxury travel experiences in the new normal.

To further enhance the appeal of his domestic properties, Trump invested in upgrading the already lavish amenities at his resorts and hotels. He understood that post-pandemic travelers were not just looking for a place to stay; they were seeking immersive, high-end experiences. Trump hotels and resorts began offering more personalized services, such as private golf lessons, luxury spa treatments, and exclusive dining experiences with renowned chefs. These offerings, tailored to the desires of affluent travelers, ensured that Trump's properties remained competitive in a market where experience was king.

In addition to the domestic market, Trump sought to reignite the international side of his hospitality business. Even with travel restrictions in place, he anticipated that the demand for luxury international travel would rebound strongly once borders reopened. His flagship international properties, such as the Trump International Hotel & Tower in Vancouver and Trump Turnberry in Scotland, remained critical to his global hospitality strategy. Trump understood that these properties represented more than just real estate; they were global landmarks that attracted elite travelers from around the world. To ensure that these properties would be ready for the post-pandemic travel boom, Trump initiated a series of renovations and upgrades to keep them in line with the latest luxury trends.

For example, Trump Turnberry, already one of the world's premier golf resorts, underwent further enhancements to its courses, making it an even more attractive destination for high-profile golf tournaments. Trump recognized that golf remained a key pillar of his hospitality empire, with his resorts regularly hosting elite players and tournaments. Golf also provided a unique advantage during the pandemic, as it allowed for outdoor recreation while maintaining social distancing. By leaning into this aspect of his business, Trump was able to keep his resorts not only open but thriving, even as other parts of the hospitality industry struggled.

At the same time, Trump saw potential in expanding his brand into new markets, particularly in regions that were less affected by political polarization. His team began negotiating deals for new hotel and resort developments in countries that remained receptive to the Trump name, such as the Middle East and Southeast Asia. Trump's vision was to create luxury destinations in emerging markets where his brand could stand out and capitalize on the growing demand for high-end travel experiences in those regions. By strategically positioning his brand in these developing luxury markets, Trump sought to further diversify his portfolio and lessen his dependence on the more politically charged American and European markets.

Technology also played a significant role in Trump's strategy to revitalize his hospitality empire. Understanding the increasing importance of digital platforms in the post-pandemic travel landscape, Trump invested in enhancing the online presence of his properties. His hotels and resorts implemented advanced digital booking systems, virtual concierge services, and interactive online tours, making it easier for high-end clients to plan and customize their stays. These digital innovations were particularly important as more travelers began relying on technology to make decisions about where to travel and how to ensure their safety.

Trump also emphasized exclusivity in his reimagined hospitality strategy. By focusing on attracting ultra-wealthy clients who valued privacy and bespoke experiences, his properties were able to thrive despite the broader downturn in the travel industry. Special memberships and invitation-only events became more prominent at his resorts, allowing Trump to create an air of exclusivity that appealed to his target market. Whether it was private golf tournaments, celebrity-hosted galas, or luxury wellness retreats, Trump's properties positioned themselves as the ultimate destinations for those seeking both opulence and privacy.

Overall, Trump's approach to expanding and revitalizing his hospitality empire was a calculated blend of adapting to new market realities and reinforcing the luxurious image that had always been the hallmark of the Trump brand. By upgrading his properties, expanding into new international markets, and embracing technology, Trump positioned his hotels and resorts to remain competitive in the ever-evolving luxury travel industry. As travel began to rebound, Trump's hospitality empire was ready to welcome back its elite clientele, offering them unparalleled luxury experiences, just as it had always done.

Reinventing Golf and Leisure Destinations

Golf has always been a central pillar of Donald Trump's business empire, and after returning to the private sector, he took the opportunity to further elevate his portfolio of golf courses and leisure destinations. For Trump, golf was more than a personal passion—it was a cornerstone of his brand, representing luxury, exclusivity, and status. With the post-pandemic market emphasizing outdoor activities and more personalized leisure experiences, Trump saw an opportunity to capitalize on these trends by reinventing his golf courses and resorts to meet the evolving demands of high-end clients.

Trump's golf courses were already some of the most prestigious in the world, hosting major tournaments and attracting an elite clientele. However, Trump recognized that even the most iconic courses needed to evolve to stay relevant in a market that had been disrupted by global events. His strategy involved not only upgrading the courses themselves but also enhancing the overall experience for guests, transforming his golf resorts into comprehensive luxury destinations.

One of the key areas of focus was expanding the scope of his golf resorts to appeal to a broader audience of high-net-worth individuals, including those who might not be avid golfers but still sought an exclusive leisure experience. To achieve this, Trump invested in the development of new amenities that went beyond golf. At resorts like Trump National Doral in Miami and Trump Turnberry in Scotland, he added luxury spas, fine dining restaurants, private villas, and bespoke concierge services that catered to the lifestyle preferences of his elite clientele. By offering world-class service and accommodations, Trump aimed to create environments where guests could enjoy a full range of luxury experiences, whether they were on the golf course or indulging in a wellness retreat.

Trump also worked to position his golf resorts as destinations for high-profile events. Hosting professional golf tournaments remained a significant part of his strategy, but he also expanded the types of events held at his properties. His resorts became venues for international business conferences, celebrity charity events, and even political gatherings, reinforcing the idea that Trump golf courses were not just for recreation but also for networking, deal-making, and entertainment. This elevated the prestige of his properties, making them sought-after locations for both leisure and business, and keeping them in the global spotlight.

At the same time, Trump understood the importance of maintaining the highest standards on the golf course itself. He brought in renowned golf course architects and designers to ensure that his courses remained in top condition, incorporating the latest trends in golf course design and sustainability. Courses like Trump International Golf Links in Scotland and Trump National Golf Club in Bedminster were meticulously maintained and enhanced to offer the best playing experience possible, while also incorporating environmentally sustainable practices. Trump knew that his clientele expected nothing but the best, and maintaining the quality of his courses was crucial to keeping his brand at the forefront of the luxury golf market.

One of the more innovative aspects of Trump's strategy was his focus on creating private, member-only golf experiences. In an era where exclusivity was more prized than ever, Trump began offering ultra-elite memberships that provided access to not just one but multiple Trump golf courses around the world. These memberships came with tailored services, such as private jet transport between courses, personalized golf coaching, and access to members-only events. For high-net-worth individuals, this level of exclusivity offered a sense of prestige and belonging to a select group, further enhancing the allure of the Trump brand.

International expansion also played a key role in Trump's reinvention of his golf and leisure business. While his properties in the United States remained iconic, Trump began eyeing new markets where golf was growing in popularity, particularly in the Middle East and Asia. These regions, with their growing number of affluent individuals and interest in luxury sports, provided fertile ground for new developments. Trump International Golf Club in Dubai, for example, became a flagship property in the region, attracting international clientele and cementing Trump's brand as a global leader in luxury golf.

Beyond the courses and the properties themselves, Trump understood the power of creating a lifestyle brand around his golf ventures. His resorts became destinations not just for golf, but for an entire luxury lifestyle that included fashion, leisure, and high society. Trump-branded golf apparel and accessories became popular among the elite, further embedding his name in the culture of luxury sports. The Trump Golf brand, like his real estate empire, was designed to be synonymous with opulence and prestige, appealing to those who sought the best in every aspect of life.

By reinventing his golf courses and leisure destinations, Trump positioned his properties to thrive in the post-pandemic world. His emphasis on exclusivity, luxury, and creating comprehensive leisure experiences allowed his brand to stay relevant in a competitive market. As outdoor activities and personalized luxury became more sought after, Trump's golf resorts stood out as destinations that offered more than just a game of golf—they offered an entire lifestyle experience tailored to the most discerning clientele. This approach ensured that Trump's golf and leisure empire remained one of the most prestigious in the world, continuing to attract the rich and powerful, just as it had throughout his career.

Conclusion

A Legacy of Bold Entrepreneurship

Donald J. Trump's journey through the business world is a testament to bold ambition, relentless drive, and a keen understanding of the power of branding. His entrepreneurial legacy is marked by both staggering successes and well-publicized challenges, but through it all, Trump has remained a dominant figure in the global business landscape. From his roots in New York City's real estate sector to his global expansion into hotels, resorts, golf courses, and media, Trump built an empire that left an indelible mark on industries far beyond the world of property development.

One of the defining traits of Trump's success is his willingness to take risks. Whether it was entering the high-stakes world of Manhattan real estate in the 1970s, venturing into the casino business in Atlantic City, or launching his brand into the world of reality television with *The Apprentice*, Trump consistently placed bold bets on opportunities that others might have overlooked or deemed too risky. His instinct for recognizing potential, particularly in distressed or undervalued assets, allowed him to turn opportunities that were fraught with uncertainty into lucrative successes. Trump's strategic gamble on Manhattan's Commodore Hotel in the 1970s is a prime example of his ability to see value where others saw decline, transforming it into the iconic Grand Hyatt and marking his arrival as a major force in real estate.

Equally integral to Trump's success has been his mastery of branding. The name "Trump" became more than just a family legacy—it became a global symbol of luxury, success, and exclusivity. Trump understood that in a crowded marketplace, brand differentiation was key, and he worked tirelessly to craft an image of opulence and high standards. From his towering skyscrapers to his luxury golf courses and five-star hotels, the Trump brand was synonymous with success. His use of media, particularly through *The Apprentice*, further cemented his identity as a master dealmaker, allowing him to reach a global audience and grow his brand far beyond the confines of real estate. Through television, Trump became both a business mogul and a pop culture icon.

Yet Trump's entrepreneurial legacy is not without its challenges. He faced numerous financial setbacks, from the struggles of his Atlantic City casinos to the broader economic downturns that impacted his businesses. However, Trump's resilience and ability to pivot in the face of adversity became central to his narrative as a businessman. He often used crises as opportunities to restructure, refocus, and rebrand. His willingness to embrace reinvention, whether by expanding into new industries or refocusing his efforts after financial hardships, is a critical lesson in staying adaptable in the ever-changing world of business.

At the heart of Trump's success is his ability to navigate complex financial landscapes, utilizing partnerships, licensing deals, and branding strategies to maximize returns with minimal risk to his personal capital. The structure of his deals, often relying on leveraging his brand without overexposing himself financially, allowed Trump to scale his empire at a pace that would have been difficult with more conventional investment approaches. His unique business model of licensing the Trump name to developments around the world enabled rapid global expansion with limited direct involvement in the operational aspects of each project. This approach not only diversified his income streams but also extended his influence to markets as far-flung as Dubai, South Korea, and Scotland.

In reflecting on Trump's entrepreneurial journey, several key strategies emerge as the foundation of his long-term success: his instinct for recognizing value in unconventional opportunities, his fearless approach to taking risks, his strategic use of branding, and his ability to navigate financial crises with creativity and resilience. These traits, along with his larger-than-life personality and relentless self-promotion, have made Trump one of the most recognizable figures in modern business.

The impact of Donald Trump's business legacy reaches far beyond the individual properties and projects that bear his name. His influence on the real estate industry, his pioneering use of personal branding, and his ability to leverage media to bolster his business ventures have all set precedents for future generations of entrepreneurs. Trump's business philosophy—centered around thinking big, embracing risk, and never backing down from a challenge—continues to inspire and provoke debate in boardrooms, classrooms, and business circles around the world.

In many ways, Trump's legacy is one of paradox. He is a figure who has both succeeded spectacularly and faced significant hurdles, yet he has always managed to remain at the forefront of public attention, using every victory and setback as a platform to further build his brand. His career is a case study in how persistence, branding, and a bold vision can create an empire that transcends industries, even in the face of adversity. As the business world continues to evolve, Donald J. Trump's approach to entrepreneurship—unconventional, bold, and unyielding—will remain a subject of fascination and study for generations to come.

Appendix: Timeline of Key Business Ventures

1970s: Early Ventures and Manhattan Real Estate

- **1971**: Donald J. Trump becomes president of his father's company, Elizabeth Trump & Son, and renames it the Trump Organization.
- **1974**: Trump negotiates a deal to acquire an option on the *Commodore Hotel* in Manhattan, which would become the *Grand Hyatt*, his first major Manhattan project.
- **1978**: Trump signs a deal with the Hyatt Hotel Corporation to develop the Grand Hyatt, securing public subsidies for the renovation project. This marks his rise as a prominent figure in New York real estate.

1980s: Building the Trump Brand

- **1983**: *Trump Tower* opens on Fifth Avenue in New York City. The skyscraper serves as Trump's headquarters and is a symbol of his luxury brand.
- **1985**: Trump purchases *Mar-a-Lago*, a historic estate in Palm Beach, Florida, which later becomes his private residence and social club.
- **1986**: Trump acquires *40 Wall Street*, one of Manhattan's tallest skyscrapers, further solidifying his presence in New York's financial district.

- **1987**: Trump publishes *The Art of the Deal*, which becomes a bestseller and positions him as a business and media personality.
- **1988**: Trump buys the *Plaza Hotel* in New York for $407.5 million, a high-profile acquisition, although the hotel eventually faces financial difficulties.

1990s: Casinos, Financial Challenges, and Reinvention

- **1990**: The *Trump Taj Mahal* casino opens in Atlantic City, billed as the "eighth wonder of the world." However, it struggles financially, leading to debt restructuring.
- **1991**: Trump's Atlantic City casino businesses, including the Taj Mahal, file for bankruptcy due to high levels of debt.
- **1995**: Trump creates the *Trump Hotels & Casino Resorts*, taking the company public. This gives him access to capital to invest in his casino properties despite their financial struggles.
- **1996**: Trump acquires *Miss Universe, Miss USA, and Miss Teen USA* pageants, expanding his media portfolio.

2000s: Media Dominance and Global Expansion

- **2001**: Trump completes the *Trump World Tower* near the United Nations in New York, one of the world's tallest residential buildings at the time.
- **2003**: *The Apprentice* debuts on NBC, becoming a massive television hit. The phrase "You're fired" becomes synonymous with Trump, and the show cements his status as a global media personality.
- **2004**: Trump launches the *Trump University*, an educational program offering real estate and entrepreneurship training. (The venture later faces legal challenges.)

- **2005**: Trump opens *Trump International Hotel & Tower Chicago*, a luxury skyscraper that quickly becomes a landmark in the city.
- **2006**: Trump enters the golf business with the acquisition of *Trump National Golf Club* in Bedminster, New Jersey. This marks the beginning of Trump's expansion into luxury golf resorts worldwide.

2010s: Global Brand Expansion and Political Ventures

- **2011**: Trump opens the *Trump International Hotel & Tower Toronto*, his first major project in Canada.
- **2012**: Trump acquires *Doonbeg Golf Club* in Ireland, adding to his portfolio of international golf resorts.
- **2014**: Trump purchases *Trump Turnberry* in Scotland, a renowned golf resort, further solidifying his global presence in the leisure industry.
- **2016**: Trump is elected the 45th President of the United States, taking a leave from his business ventures during his term.

2020s: Return to Business and Continued Expansion

- **2021**: After leaving office, Trump returns to his business empire, refocusing on his real estate, branding, and golf course ventures. His properties, including *Mar-a-Lago* and *Trump National Golf Clubs*, continue to serve as high-profile destinations for his supporters and business associates.
- **2022**: Trump expands his golf resort operations, investing further in his international properties, including *Trump International Golf Links* in Scotland and *Trump International Golf Club* in Dubai.

This timeline illustrates Donald Trump's diverse ventures across industries, highlighting both his bold moves and ability to navigate challenges while building a global brand that endures across decades.

References

1. **Books:**
   - Trump, Donald J., and Tony Schwartz. *The Art of the Deal*. New York: Random House, 1987.
   - Blair, Gwenda. *The Trumps: Three Generations That Built an Empire*. New York: Simon & Schuster, 2000.
   - O'Brien, Timothy L. *TrumpNation: The Art of Being the Donald*. New York: Warner Books, 2005.
   - Trump, Donald J. *Trump: The Art of the Comeback*. New York: Times Books, 1997.
   - Barrett, Wayne. *Trump: The Deals and the Downfall*. New York: HarperCollins, 1992.
2. **Articles:**
   - Haberman, Maggie. "The President Who Never Stops Talking." *The New York Times*, March 2018.
   - Davidson, Adam. "Donald Trump's Business Career is a Remarkably Successful Failure." *The New Yorker*, May 23, 2016.
   - Bruni, Frank. "The Myth of Trump's Business Genius." *The New York Times*, August 12, 2016.
   - Schwartz, Tony. "I Wrote 'The Art of the Deal' with Donald Trump. His Self-Sabotage is Rooted in His Past." *The Washington Post*, July 18, 2016.
   - Fisher, Marc. "Donald Trump and Atlantic City: A Story of Entrepreneurial Success and Failure." *The Washington Post*, June 27, 2016.
3. **Interviews:**
   - Trump, Donald J. Interview by David Letterman. *Late Show with David Letterman*. CBS, November 19, 2007.

- Trump, Donald J. Interview by Larry King. *Larry King Live*. CNN, August 26, 2004.
- Schwartz, Tony. Interview with Jane Mayer. *The New Yorker*, July 25, 2016.
- Trump, Donald J. Interview by Howard Stern. *The Howard Stern Show*. SiriusXM Radio, April 3, 2005.

4. **Business Publications:**

- "Trump Tower: The Ultimate Deal." *Forbes*, February 1983.
- "Donald Trump's Biggest Real Estate Projects." *The Real Deal*, September 2015.
- "Donald Trump and the Plaza Hotel." *The New York Times*, August 14, 1988.
- "The World of Trump: A Timeline of His Real Estate Projects." *Business Insider*, October 2020.
- "The Trump Organization's Global Reach." *Financial Times*, July 15, 2016.

5. **Websites:**

- The Trump Organization. "About the Trump Organization." https://www.trump.com/about.
- NBC News. "Timeline of Donald Trump's Biggest Business Ventures." https://www.nbcnews.com/news/donald-trump-business-timeline.

6. **Documentaries and Media:**

- *Trump: What's the Deal?* Directed by Al Levin, 1991.
- *American Experience: The President*. PBS, 2017. Documentary series detailing the history of U.S. presidents and their business ventures.
- *The Apprentice*. NBC Television Series, 2004–2015.

This comprehensive list of sources provides an in-depth understanding of Donald Trump's business ventures and the many aspects of his career. These references cover his early real estate developments, his rise as a media personality, and his global brand expansion.

Milton Keynes UK
Ingram Content Group UK Ltd.
UKHW040308181024
449757UK00005B/407